Whoever thought  rm that Bill Farley de   t is essential for grow   ery Christian benefits   s of what God has done for us in Christ, and this involves reflection on some of the most glorious teachings of Scripture that span from eternity past to eternity future. Such is the breadth of the gospel, and such is the opportunity for Christians to have their minds and hearts transformed by the gospel's power. Those who read this book will enter into this gospel breadth with the hope and promise of greater love for God and longing to live in the fullness of the gospel.

> **—Bruce A. Ware,** Professor of Christian Theology, The Southern Baptist Theological Seminary, Louisville, Kentucky

Bill Farley continues his valuable contributions to gospel-centered living with *Hidden in the Gospel.* While others have mentioned the importance of preaching to ourselves, Bill shows us how to do so. His practical unpacking of the primary theological components of a "wide-angle" understanding of the biblical gospel is just what we need to keep our self-talk grounded in God's redemptive work in Christ. I am confident this book will be useful to all believers, whether for individual study or in a group setting.

> **—Randal Roberts,** President and Professor of Spiritual Formation, Western Seminary, Portland, Oregon

Pastor-theologian Bill Farley has given us a grand tool for sustaining and elevating our souls by preaching the massive gospel of Christ to, of all people, *ourselves!* This small gem of a book provides a joyous gospel feast that begins with our election in

Christ before the foundation of the world and ends with Christ's new creation. No small thoughts here! This is the recipe for big, expansive, and ever-expanding hearts.

> —**R. Kent Hughes,** Senior Pastor Emeritus, College Church in Wheaton

Pastors would have to engage in very little counseling if Christians prioritized what Bill Farley exhorts his readers to do in *Hidden in the Gospel.* To gain clarity on the gospel of Jesus Christ and to practice consistent self-talk based upon that gospel would transform the lives of Christians, their homes, and their churches.

> —**Don Whitney,** Associate Professor of Biblical Spirituality, Senior Associate Dean for the School of Theology, The Southern Baptist Theological Seminary, Louisville, Kentucky

Hidden in the Gospel

Truths **You Forget to Tell Yourself** Every Day

WILLIAM P. FARLEY

P U B L I S H I N G

P.O. BOX 817 • PHILLIPSBURG • NEW JERSEY 08865-0817

Dedicated to Ken Fry and Johnny Masis.

Their love for the gospel, and their encouragement, inspired me to write on this idea.

ISBN: 978-1-59638-746-1 (pbk)
ISBN: 978-1-59638-747-8 (ePub)
ISBN: 978-1-59638-748-5 (Mobi)

Printed in the United States of America

Library of Congress Control Number: 2013921303

Contents

Preface

This is a book about basic Christian doctrines, with an emphasis on practical application.

I have written it with the conviction that theology matters. However, theology separated from real life is not helpful. It is just dry, crusty religion. Who wants that? On the other hand, attempts to apply the Christian life without clear-cut, sharply defined theology will usually end up in legalism. No one wants that either. What really changes believers is clearly defined theology driven deep into the heart by the power of the Holy Spirit. It produces love, joy, and peace. That is the goal of every Christian, and it is also the goal of this book.

In other words, you are holding a book in your hands about basic theology for everyday Christians like you and me. It is a book about the most fundamental doctrine—the gospel—and why we should daily preach it to ourselves. That raises an important question. Why another book about the gospel? More pointedly, why a book about preaching the gospel to oneself? This topic is not new.

The church needs this book for at least two reasons. First, we need to preach a bigger gospel. The gospel is more, but never less, than justification by faith alone. In addition, it is more, but never less, than penal substitution. This book is about what I will call a wide-angle gospel. By "wide-angle" I mean it is about all that God the Father has done to save us, starting in eternity past and moving forward to eternity future. I am not aware of any books that exhort Christians to preach a wide-angle gospel to themselves.

There is a second reason that this book matters. I don't know of any books that connect preaching the gospel to yourself with daily life application.

I was a Christian for at least twenty-five years before I first heard the words "Preach the gospel to yourself!" Looking back, I wish I had heard that message earlier. This concept has been decisive in my Christian maturation. At first it meant, "Remind yourself regularly that Jesus died for you, that he loves you, that he forgives you, and that you are saved by faith plus nothing." Then it began to morph into something bigger and more beautiful. As the years have progressed, the meaning and application of the gospel have expanded. The applications to my own life, and to the lives of people in my congregation, have grown and multiplied. I have written this book to share my joy with you, the reader, and also to motivate you to go beyond this little book in your knowledge of, and application of, the gospel.

THE GOSPEL IS THEOLOGY

Christians get their theology—their understanding of who God is and what he is like—primarily from the gospel. The gospel, culminating in the death and resurrection of Christ, reveals God. It unveils him. The unveiling is always shocking. God is not what we expect. However, after the shock wears off, we find God infinitely better than we expect.

This book is about how to know God through the gospel story. It is about the joy that proceeds from getting to know God through the discipline of talking back to yourself—what some have called "preaching the gospel to yourself."

This book is not a comprehensive analysis of the many doctrines that make up the gospel. For example, I do not cover Pentecost. Instead, each chapter covers one of the events that form the matrix of the gospel.

It is also important to note that this book does not treat these truths comprehensively. For example, chapter 5 surveys the doctrine of the atonement in only three thousand words. An informed writer could spend three thousand pages on this subject and not exhaust it. Rather, this book is an attempt to help the reader connect some of the crucial gospel doctrines with their *application to daily life*. In other words, this book is an attempt to help you feed on Jesus by going deeper with the gospel.

FEEDING ON JESUS

At the Last Supper,

> Jesus took bread, and after blessing it broke it and gave it to the disciples, and said, "Take, eat; this is my body." And he took a cup, and when he had given thanks he gave it to them, saying, "Drink of it, all of you, for this is my blood of the covenant, which is poured out for many for the forgiveness of sins." (Matt. 26:26–28)

The body and blood of Christ represent the heart of the gospel event, the cross of Christ. In other words, just as bread and wine sustain physical life, so eating Jesus' body and drinking his blood sustain spiritual life. If I don't eat bread, my body will die. If I don't feed on Jesus, my spiritual life will die.

The context of Jesus' command is the gospel. The bread is Christ's body, broken on the cross. The wine is his shed blood. In other words, the Lord's Supper is a reminder of what Jesus *did* for us, and we are commanded to feed on it daily.

Most of us eat at least three meals a day (sometimes with snacks in between). In the same way, God wants us to feed on Christ by feeding on the gospel. We do this by preaching (meditating on) the gospel to ourselves throughout the day.

Jesus expressed this idea in another way. "Abide in me, and I in you. As the branch cannot bear fruit by itself, unless it abides in the vine, neither can you, unless you abide in me" (John 15:4). *To abide* means literally "to dwell in." We dwell in Christ by abiding in the truths of the gospel. Those who do so become increasingly fruitful!

7

THREE SPIRITUAL TREASURES

In addition, God enriches those who cultivate this discipline in at least three ways. First, they progressively get to know God—I mean, they really come to know him. The gospel makes God's justice exquisite. The gospel glorifies his mercy and grace. The gospel makes God's wrath terrible, but then God's wrath makes the love of God inexpressibly precious. The gospel shows us the absolute sovereignty of God, but it does so without diminishing our responsibility. The gospel magnifies the horror of human sin, but it salves that knowledge with God's grace and compassion. We could go on and on.

Second, the gospel motivates their sanctification. The more you know God (theology), the more you will want to imitate him. The more you gaze upon the glory of Christ through the window of the gospel, the more you will long to be like him. That was what Paul had in mind when he wrote, "And we all, with unveiled face, beholding the glory of the Lord, are being transformed into the same image from one degree of glory to another. For this comes from the Lord who is the Spirit" (2 Cor. 3:18). The glory of God shines most clearly through the gospel truths discussed in these chapters.

Third, the gospel defines God's will. The gospel is our ethic. It shows us how to live. Although each chapter of this book will make practical applications, my fervent hope is that you will go deeper and apply the gospel to every area of your life—your marriage, your parenting, and how you relate to your peers on Monday morning. A recommended reading list is at the end of each chapter for those who want to explore the material in that chapter in more depth.

I have written this book to be used in a variety of settings. The chapters are intentionally short. New Christians, unbelievers who want to understand basic Christian doctrine, and long-time saints who want to know how to apply the gospel constitute my target audience. I have placed study questions at the end of each chapter to facilitate small group reading and discussion.

Preach to Yourself

I sat down in a comfortable seat at a local coffee shop with a hot cup of "Joe" to do some reading. Seated across from me was a young woman deeply engrossed in a book. Sensing we might have something in common, I struck up a conversation.

"I notice you're reading Dr. Martyn Lloyd-Jones."

"Yes, I'm reading *Spiritual Depression*. It is one of my favorite books. Are you familiar with it?"

"I finished it a few months ago. What chapter are you on?"

"Actually," she said, "I've read it three times."

"Well, I'm a pastor," I confessed. "And *Spiritual Depression* has helped many in my congregation."

"Before I read this book, I was in the habit of listening to my fears and doubts," she answered. "But now I preach to myself. This concept has changed my life."

As she said this, I remembered "the Doctor's" exhortation at the end of the first chapter. "I say that we must talk to ourselves instead of allowing 'ourselves' to talk to us! Do you realize what that means? I suggest the main trouble in this whole matter of spiritual depression in a sense is this, that we allow our self to talk to us instead of talking to our self."[1]

Lloyd-Jones was on to something. It is a key to robust spiritual experience. We can either listen to ourselves—our fears, doubts, insecurities, hurts, and failures—or we can preach to ourselves. Maturing believers cultivate the discipline of preaching to themselves. In fact, they turn this into an art form. They read Scripture, internalize it, and then continually preach its truths back to themselves. When fears of death and dying arise, they speak to themselves about the world to come. When guilt grips their heart, they remind themselves that they have been united with Christ and that Christ's righteousness is theirs. They don't listen to self. They preach to self!

What do I mean by preaching to self? First, it is more than Scripture memorization. Scripture memorization is an important discipline. However, you can memorize the Bible but never cultivate the discipline of preaching to yourself. Individual verses seldom sum up the big picture that we so desperately need.

Preaching to self also differs radically from positive thinking. Truth is often irrelevant to the positive thinker. Instead, he or she tries to create reality by thinking positively. *I can become whatever I affirm. Reality is irrelevant. I am wonderful and talented. Whether I really am makes no difference. But if I say this enough, I will believe it and become it.*

However, when a Christian preaches to himself, he presumes just the opposite. He does not manufacture truth with affirmations. He cannot create reality. Instead, his affirmations reflect the immutable Reality that is really there. It alone changes lives. In other words, Christians do not create truth. The Truth creates the Christian. It shapes and molds us. Someday we will give an accounting to the God who is the ultimate Reality.

The contention of this little book is that Lloyd-Jones was right. It also contends that there is one truth that matters more than all the others combined, and the Christian should preach it to himself on a regular basis. It is the gospel, the most fundamental Christian reality.

Jack Miller (1928–1996) first popularized the idea of preaching the gospel to oneself. A Presbyterian church planter in Philadelphia, a seminary professor, and a prolific author,

Miller was thoroughly gospel centered. He saw the centrality of the gospel to all of life. In Miller's view, the gospel was not just a subject for new believers. The gospel was crucial for the progressive sanctification of all believers at all stages of their spiritual journey.

In his book *The Discipline of Grace*, Jerry Bridges popularized Miller's idea. Bridges exhorts his readers to preach the gospel to themselves. For Bridges, this means a solid focus on what happened at the cross.

> To preach the gospel to yourself, then, means that you continually face up to your own sinfulness and then flee to Jesus through faith in His shed blood and righteous life. It means that you appropriate, again by faith, the fact that Jesus fully satisfied the law of God, that He is your propitiation, and that God's holy wrath is no longer directed toward you.[2]

The book you are holding is a tutorial on how to preach the gospel to yourself. I am shamelessly and unapologetically building on the ideas of men like Lloyd-Jones, Miller, and Bridges. But I am also speaking from personal experience. I have discovered the benefit of continually preaching the gospel to myself. It has melted the fog of depression, repulsed the demons of despair, and displaced feelings of unworthiness and failure with the love of God. When I have been discouraged, it has motivated me to keep plodding. It has humbled me before the wonder of God's glorious grace. It has encouraged me to love God and others. It has prompted me to be patient with the failings of others. It has urged me to forgive seventy times seven times.

What do I mean by the gospel?

DEFINITIONS

I want to go back to a subject that I brought up in the preface. When we think of the gospel, we usually think of Christ's death and resurrection, and that is appropriate. Christ's death and resurrection are the heart and soul of the gospel. "The message of the atoning death of Christ for sin," note Jerry Bridges and Bob Bevington, "is the heart of [the apostles'] gospel and is forever to be the cornerstone of the Christian faith. . . . [It is] the central fact in all of the entire history of the world. It is the chief topic and essential truth from which they always start and to which they always return."[3]

Although I agree with Bridges and Bevington wholeheartedly, I want to go one step further. In this book, I want to take a broader view of the gospel. The English word *gospel* is a modernized version of the Middle English word *godspell*, meaning "good tale." Going back further, *godspell* is a translation of the New Testament Greek word *euangelion*, which just means "good news," usually as declared by an emperor to his subjects. The gospel is the declaration of what God—our sovereign King and Emperor—has done to rescue us from sin and its consequence, the wrath of God.

It is good news indeed! In fact, when one's plight in sin is fully understood, it is the best news anyone could possibly hear.

Using the term more broadly, the gospel is good news about all that God has done in Christ to save sinners and redeem the cosmos from the effects of sin. It includes our election before the foundation of the world, Christ's incarnation, his active obedience, his substitutionary death, his resurrection and ascension, Pentecost, and the final judgment. It also includes the hope of a new creation purged of sin and infused with the active presence of God.

Although the gospel commands us to respond with faith and repentance, it is not fundamentally about what we should do. The gospel is about something that God has done. "The gospel is objective," notes Jeff Purswell. "It tells us what God has done to save his people."[4] Or, in the words of the *New Bible Dictionary*, the gospel is "the good news that God in Jesus Christ has fulfilled his promises to Israel, and that a way of salvation has been opened to all."[5]

In other words, thinking of the gospel in this way is like seeing it through a wide-angle camera lens. It is bigger than Christ's death and resurrection. It includes what God did for us in eternity past and what God still plans to do for us in eternity future.[6]

Why the gospel and not some other truth? There is no subject more important to preach to oneself. It is the story line of Scripture. It is the central theme of the Bible. The Old Testament predicts and looks forward to the gospel. Matthew, Mark, Luke, and John record the central facts of the gospel—Christ's life, death, and resurrection. Acts records the efforts of the early church to export the gospel. The Epistles explain and apply the gospel. The Bible is all about the gospel!

In addition, the gospel is the Bible's unifying theme. Some don't think the Bible has a unifying theme.[7] Others find it in the many covenants throughout Scripture. Some find it in prophecy or the millennial hope. However, I am convinced that the Bible does have a unifying theme and that it is knowable. But if we aren't careful, we can miss the forest because we are so engrossed in the trees. The gospel is so obviously the center of the Bible's story that it's often assumed and subsequently overlooked.

Last, it is through the gospel that God achieves his ultimate end. The glory of God is the ultimate end of all things, and the gospel is the means through which God glorifies himself. It is how he achieves his ends.[8]

The cross of Christ is the focal point of the gospel. It is the heart and soul of the gospel. Why? Because Christ's suffering and death on the cross, more than any other event in history, displays before our eyes the glory of God. There we see the love of God hidden in his wrath, the mercy of God concealed in his justice, and the grace of God displayed through the demands of his holiness. In addition, we see ourselves. We see the horror of our sin. We see our failings as God sees them.

This book will look at several crucial aspects of the gospel. Each chapter will explain one aspect of the gospel and then answer the question, "So what?" It will conclude with an example of how to preach this truth to yourself. Starting with election in eternity past, we will progress to Christ's incarnation. Then we will examine his sinless life, his substitutionary death, his resurrection from the dead, his ascension into heaven, his return in glory to judge the living and the dead, and finally our ultimate hope, the new heavens and the new earth, which Peter referred to as the "restoration of all things" (Acts 3:21 NKJV).

BENEFITS

Why should you read this book? Cultivating the discipline of preaching the gospel to yourself has many benefits. Let's close this chapter with seven.

First of all, it regularly and repetitively exposes us to the glory of God. Moses wanted to know God's essential nature, so he screwed up his courage and asked to see God's glory, but God replied, "You cannot see my face, for man shall not see me and live" (Ex. 33:20). However, the next day God passed by and declared to Moses what he was not allowed to see. "The LORD, the LORD, a God merciful and gracious, slow to anger, and abounding in steadfast love and faithfulness, keeping steadfast love for thousands, forgiving iniquity and transgression and sin, but who will by no means clear the guilty, visiting the iniquity of the fathers on the children and the children's children, to the third and the fourth generation" (Ex. 34:6–7). What a glorious verbal picture of God's moral beauty. Here we have mercy, grace, steadfast love, faithfulness, and forgiveness all coupled with a strict observance of God's perfect justice.

The staggering promise of the new covenant is that God has made available, in a way that we can see and survive, a glimpse of that glory. We see it, not with our physical eyes, but with the eyes of our heart. That is the essence of new birth. God

14

"has shone in our hearts to give the light of the knowledge of the glory of God in the face of Jesus Christ" (2 Cor. 4:6).

God has displayed this "glory" through the gospel, and meditation is a key that unlocks it. The best way to meditate is to preach the gospel to oneself regularly. "To behold the glory of Christ in the gospel is a discipline," writes Jerry Bridges. "It is a habit we must develop by practice as we learn to preach the gospel to ourselves every day."[9] This is what Paul has in mind when he tells us to "seek the things that are above" and "set your minds on things that are above" (Col. 3:1–2).

There is a second reason to preach the gospel to yourself. It will help you grow in humility. On the cross, Jesus takes our place. He gets what we deserve, and it is ugly. In a previous book, *Gospel-Powered Humility*, I made this point. When many people hear the word *humility*, negative thoughts come to mind. Who wants to be humbled? But those with spiritual wisdom beg God to humble them. They know that most of God's riches flow through the funnel of humility. God gives grace to the humble (James 4:6). What does this grace look like? How does it come to us? Here are some examples: intimacy with Christ (Isa. 57:15), favor with God (Prov. 3:34), exaltation by God (Ps. 147:6), salvation in the broadest sense (Matt. 5:3), and honor from God (Prov. 15:33). These are all manifestations of God's grace to those growing in humility. "The good news of Jesus is not intended to make us feel good about ourselves," notes Ed Welch. "Instead, the good news humbles us."[10]

Third, those who preach the gospel to themselves are most likely to gain deliverance from that three-headed monster—guilt, inferiority, and low self-image. Here is the reason. The gospel is all about grace. Grace is reward given to those who deserve punishment. The gospel is the good news that God loves us not because of our virtues. He loves us in spite of their absence. The gospel is about divine power flowing through weak people. It is about the exaltation of God's wisdom through foolish people. It is about God using the lowly and despised to shame the important. In other words, the gospel is for the needy, the guilty, and those who feel inferior. The gospel increasingly dissolves guilt, inferiority, and despair in the solvent of God's love.

Fourth, preaching the gospel to oneself accelerates sanctification. *Sanctification* is just a big word meaning "growth in godliness." As Paul David Tripp writes, "No one is more influential in your life than you are, because no one else talks to you more."[11] What you say to yourself will influence you more than all the sermons you hear, all the counseling you receive, and all the Bible reading you do.

A right understanding of the gospel provides motivation for developing love, compassion, and grace toward others. Yes, the gospel is a message for unbelievers. But, as we have seen, it is also the most important motivator for growing holiness. John Piper writes, "Our temptation is to think that the gospel is for beginners and then we go on to greater things. But the real challenge is to see the gospel as the greatest thing—and getting greater all the time."[12]

Fifth, those who repeatedly preach the gospel to themselves are increasingly "abounding in thanksgiving" (Col. 2:6). Why? The gospel shows us what we deserve—judgment. But, here is the good news: because of the gospel, we will never get what we deserve. No matter how bad our circumstances are, this truth will make us overflow with gratitude. The gospel reminds us that Christians are not getting, and never will get, what they deserve. Believers who preach the gospel to themselves understand this. Therefore, they are increasingly thankful, and thankful people are joyful people.

Sixth, those who preach the gospel to themselves are increasingly hopeful. That is because the gospel culminates in a new heaven and a new earth—a future utopia that God has promised to bring to pass. It is about "Paradise restored." The future for every Christian is an eternity with no crying, nor mourning, nor pain.

Finally, preaching the gospel to oneself culminates in worship. The gospel is the ultimate ground for worship. Revelation 5 paints a picture of the worship that is taking place in heaven as you read these words. At the center of that worship is the Lamb who was slain, now standing in victory. What is the response? Heaven spontaneously erupts in a glorious, noisy, ecstatic worship. There is clapping, shouting, and singing. Every step toward the gospel takes us closer to the infinite goodness of the infinite God. That is why the gospel provokes grateful worship.

I preach the gospel to myself when I am shaving, when I am driving, when I am discouraged, and when I am in a place of deep comfort. Most importantly, I preach the gospel to myself after failure, which is all too often. I have written this book with the hope that you will do likewise.

"To really hear the Gospel," notes Mark Dever, "is to be shaken to your core. To really hear the Gospel is to change."[13]

That is my hope for you as you read this book.

Discussion Questions

1. In your own words, what was the main point of this chapter?

2. What was your favorite passage from this chapter? Why?

3. What does it mean to listen to oneself? What things do you hear when your self is speaking?

4. By contrast, what does it mean to preach to oneself? What kinds of truth should you preach to yourself?

5. What comes to mind when you hear the word *gospel*?

6. In your own words, explain the difference between a wide-angle gospel and a narrow-angle gospel.

7. What are some of the doctrines that this author includes in the wide-angle gospel?

8. In light of this chapter, what would repentance look like?

Further Reading

- Bridges, Jerry. *The Discipline of Grace: God's Role and Our Role in the Pursuit of Holiness*. Colorado Springs: NavPress, 2006. See esp. chap. 3, "Preach the Gospel to Yourself."

- Edwards, Jonathan. *Religious Affections*. New York: Shepard Kollock, 1787. Available online at http://www.jonathan-edwards.org/ReligiousAffections.pdf.

- Gilbert, Greg. *What Is the Gospel?* Wheaton, IL: Crossway, 2010.

- Greear, J. D. *Gospel: Recovering the Power that Made Christianity Revolutionary*. Nashville: B&H, 2011.

- Whitney, Donald S. *Spiritual Disciplines for the Christian Life*. Colorado Springs: NavPress, 1991. See esp. chaps. 2 and 3, "Bible Intake (Parts 1 and 2)".

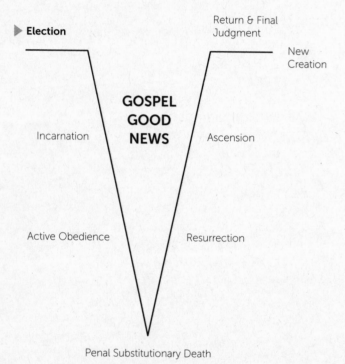

Chosen before the Foundation of the World

The good news of the gospel begins in eternity past with the doctrine of election.

Whenever I think of election, I think of the TV series from the late fifties called *The Millionaire*. I have fond grade-school memories of our family gathered around our black and white TV enjoying that week's new episode. Each week introduced the story of someone to whom the fabulously wealthy John Beresford Tipton Jr. gave one million dollars on the condition that the beneficiary never know the identity of his benefactor.

Although you could hear his voice in the background, Tipton's face never appeared. He was a mysterious character. Instead, the show featured his executive secretary, Michael Anthony, who tracked down the astounded beneficiaries and presented each of them with a million-dollar check.

Why Tipton chose one beneficiary over another was never explained. Sometimes the recipient was poor, sometimes wealthy; sometimes a law-abiding citizen, sometimes in prison. Tipton wanted to study the recipient's reaction to an unexpected influx of wealth.

The friends and neighbors of the recipient might have been jealous, but they never blamed Tipton for not giving the money to them. Why? They knew that Tipton was not obligated to be generous. They also knew that the recipient had done nothing to merit the money. It was Tipton's money, and he was free to do with it as he wished. Instead, it was the generosity of Tipton that impressed them.

In the same way, although he had no obligation to do so, God, in love, before the foundation of the world, elected those to whom he would give the unmerited gift of saving grace. Properly understood, this doctrine is one of the most encouraging gospel truths.

EXPOSITORY EXULTATION

Although Christians often avoid or try to get around this doctrine, the Bible sees it as a reason for exuberant joy. Paul's introduction to Ephesians is a good example.

> Blessed be the God and Father of our Lord Jesus Christ, who has blessed us in Christ with every spiritual blessing in the heavenly places, even as he *chose* us in him before the foundation of the world, that we should be holy and blameless before him. In love he *predestined* us for adoption as sons through Jesus Christ, according to the purpose of his will. (Eph. 1:3–5)

In this passage, Paul discusses both God's choosing of his children (election) and predestination, but notice the context. It is one of joyful optimism. In fact, these three verses begin a long expository exultation in which Paul celebrates the Father's saving work. It runs from verse 3 to verse 14. Paul rejoices in our redemption, our adoption, the gift of the Holy Spirit, and our sanctification. But the first blessing in which he glories is God's *election* of his people. God the Father chose us in Christ before the foundation of the world. Most importantly, love motivated the Father to predestine "us for adoption as sons" (Eph. 1:5).

It is important to note that election and predestination do not depress Paul. Paul does not see this subject through the lens of pessimistic fatalism. Just the opposite. The doctrine of election is the first in a long list of blessings, coming from God the Father, that excite Paul. It motivates a torrent of joy, enthusiasm, and hope. There is no getting around the joyous context in which we find this doctrine. Why is Paul so enthusiastic? There are several reasons.

First, Paul exults in election because the saving love of God is at the heart of it. Verses 4–5 read, "In *love* he predestined us." God elects people because he delights in them. "He rescued me," writes David, "because he delighted in me" (Ps. 18:19).

Second, Paul is excited about election because he assumes that unless God elected people, no one would be saved. We are all sinners, dead in sin (Eph. 2:5). God is our enemy (Rom. 5:10). We are not seeking God. "No one seeks for God" (Rom. 3:11). This means that all of us are running away from God as fast as possible. When God elects, he reaches down to save some of those utterly unworthy creatures who are running away from him as fast as they can. No compulsion motivates him. He has no need that we can meet. Like John Beresford Tipton Jr., he is not obligated to be merciful. He elects one and not another to glorify his love to the unworthy, plain and simple.

Third, Paul is excited about election because it is the foundation for grace. One of the big themes of Ephesians is grace. That is why Paul begins this letter with election. Grace is *unmerited* favor. It is reward given to those who deserve judgment. Grace means that Christ takes the punishment we deserve, so that we can get the reward that Christ deserves. We don't get in on this by being better or trying harder. It is God's *gift*, and it is his gift to those who have no claim on his electing love.

Fourth, Paul is excited about election because Christ came to save those whom his Father had chosen from the foundation of the world. He lived a perfect life and died a criminal's death for specific people who the Father had determined, long before, to save. Jesus came to fulfill the Father's plan.

Election is central to our gospel optimism. God, who is in absolute control of everything, decided, before he created the world, who would be saved. He knows everything that will come to pass because he is in total control of all that will come to pass. This includes our salvation. For many, though, this is problematic.

DIFFERENT UNDERSTANDINGS

Because it is all over the pages of the Bible, all evangelicals believe in some version of election. You can't be serious about Scripture and ignore this subject. But sincere Christians differ on *why* God elects one and not another. Some believe that God elects one over another because he foresees their decision to believe. This is called "conditional" election. It is the belief that God conditioned my election on my decision to believe. God looked down the corridors of history and saw that I would decide to trust in Christ, so he elected me. This is what many people assume when they first believe. For many years, it was my view also, and it didn't change until I made a close study of the biblical texts.[1]

That study brought me to a better understanding. God does not elect one over another because of how good they have been. He delights in one over another just because he has decided to do so. He is the sovereign King. He owes us no explanation, and he gives us none. Election, in this view, is all of grace. As with John Beresford Tipton Jr., it is all about *unmerited* favor bestowed on totally unworthy individuals who have done nothing to merit it. This understanding is called "unconditional" election. God's choosing is not based upon any condition, any foreseen goodness (i.e., a decision to believe) in the one chosen. Just the opposite. God chooses us despite the complete absence of foreseen goodness. He chooses us not because he foresees goodness in us. He chooses to *produce* goodness in us.

The doctrine of indwelling sin is the great divide between these two views. The Christian who believes in unconditional election believes that we are "dead" in sin and by nature "children of wrath" (Eph. 2:1–3). Because we are dead in sin, Paul tells us that "no one seeks for God" (Rom. 3:11). In other words, no one would ever turn to the God of the Bible and pursue him unless God took the initiative and reached out to him first. In the words of Jesus, "No one knows the Son except the Father, and no one knows the Father except the Son and *anyone to whom the Son chooses to reveal him*" (Matt. 11:27).

Why am I including the doctrine of election in a series of meditations on the gospel? If the gospel is the story of what God has done to save us, then election is where it all began. Therefore, this is the first gospel truth we should preach to ourselves. Past generations have understood it this way. In the words of a seventeenth-century Puritan, "The doctrine of election containeth the whole sum and scope of the gospel."[2] And, in the words of a contemporary, Iain Murray, "The whole of the work of Christ, is therefore to be understood in relation to the doctrine of election, and indeed . . . it cannot be understood without it."[3]

OBJECTIONS

It would not be honest to continue without addressing the many thoughtful objections that sincere Christians have to this doctrine. I want to address the three most important ones.

The first objection is that unconditional election is not fair. Many who deserve a chance to go to heaven will go to hell, yet, through no fault of their own, they were shut out before they were even born.

This is a rational objection, except for one fact. It rests upon a faulty assumption. It assumes that we are good people, that we all *deserve* an opportunity to be saved. But the Bible teaches the opposite. It states that God owes us nothing but justice. God's grace, mercy, and love, when given, are always given to the *unworthy*, to those who deserve only justice. Therefore, if God were strictly fair, everyone would go to hell and no one would be saved.

The only one who gets unfair treatment is Christ. He was the only man who ever merited heaven. Yet, in order to save us, he bore the full weight of our sins, went to the cross, and suffered the punishment that we deserve. He did this in order that we might enjoy the eternal life that he deserves. Now that is unfair!

There is a second objection. What about the many passages that discuss God's love for all men? John 3:16 is a good example. "For God so loved the world, that he gave his only begotten Son" (KJV). The doctrine of election, however, implies that God loves only the elect. This is a rational objection. Many verses speak of God's universal love. In his book *The Difficult Doctrine of the Love of God*, D. A. Carson probably gives the best response to this problem. He suggests that we affirm God's general love for all men. He died for all, and he invites all to respond to the gospel. But the Bible also speaks about God's special, saving love for his elect. "God sets his affection on his chosen ones in a way in which he does not set his affection on others."[4]

Carson's solution is ambiguous, but I think it the best. When Scripture gives us two truths that don't seem to fit together, faithful Christians just say yes. Regarding election, there is much that we cannot understand, that we must just accept. A true Calvinist is willing to live with the tension provided by mystery.

There is a third objection. What about human responsibility? If God elects certain individuals before the foundation of the world—if those who will be saved have been determined in advance—then why pray or evangelize? Here is another mystery—the relationship between divine sovereignty and human responsibility. If you remove the face of an old pocket watch, you will observe a set of moving wheels. Some are moving clockwise; some are moving counterclockwise. At first glance, it appears that the watch is working against itself. Yet the contrary movements work together to produce an accurate timepiece.

The workings of divine sovereignty and human responsibility are similar. Both are true. God is in total control. Not one sparrow falls from the bush nor one hair from the head that God has not both foreknown and brought to pass (Matt. 10:29–30). Yet at the same time we make real choices that change things, and for them we will give an accounting on the day of judgment (2 Cor. 5:10).

Humble Christians are willing to live with mystery. God is infinite. So there must be huge areas that are beyond comprehension. Like the wheels in the watch, two concepts run through the Bible on parallel tracks—the sovereignty of God and the responsibility of man. Both are true. Although we cannot understand them, they are theologically compatible. Theologians call this the doctrine of <u>compatibilism</u>.

Compatibilism means that your salvation and the salvation of those around you have all been predetermined, yet God still hears prayer, and your prayer moves God to save the unsaved. How these things go together we cannot understand. We just rest in it. The apostles believed in election and predestination, yet no group of people ever prayed more or worked harder to evangelize the lost.

SO WHAT?

"OK, you have convinced me. But why should I make a big deal over this doctrine? Why should I cherish it? Why should I preach it to myself when the alarm clock goes off at 6:00 a.m.? Certainly this doctrine is not necessary for salvation."

You are right. Millions are saved who don't believe in unconditional election. However, it is my conviction that until you embrace unconditional election, your knowledge of God will be impoverished. In addition, you will never truly rest in the grace of God or the love of God. Your joy will be diminished. That is because election is crucial to the knowledge of God and your capacity to rest in God's grace.

What is the connection between election and the knowledge of God? God's glory is a synonym for the fullness of his goodness, and election is at the heart of God's glory. Moses' dialogue with God after the incident of the golden calf, already discussed in chapter 1, makes this clear. Moses asked to see God's glory, and here is how God responded: "'I will make all my goodness pass before you and will proclaim before you my name "The LORD." *And I will be gracious to whom I will be gracious, and will show mercy on whom I will show mercy.* But,' he said, 'you cannot see my face, for man shall not see me and live'" (Ex. 33:19–20).

At the heart of it all—at the heart of God's glory—is this sentence: "*I will be gracious to whom I will be gracious, and will show mercy on whom I will show mercy.*" In other words, God's freedom to show mercy to one rather than another is at the heart of the divine nature—that is, the goodness of God, or the glory of God.

But this is not how many of us see it. It is all about us. The sovereignty of God is way down the list. For many Christians, God is small and man is big. However, belief in unconditional election expands our view of God, and for many this is a significant and joyful adjustment. Paul's sovereign God, described in Ephesians 1, is true, satisfying, and comforting.

There is a second reason why this doctrine matters. God's freedom to elect is the foundation for biblical grace. As we have already noted, God elects not because he foresees our good works. He elects to *produce* good works. This has a tremendous effect upon our rest in God and our security in his love. If God elects me because he foresees some virtue in me—for example, faith or a disposition to seek him—then the basis of his love for me is my performance. If this is true, then unless I continue to perform, he will surely reject me. But if he elected me despite the complete absence of any performance, in spite of my numerous sins and failings, then I am eternally secure.

In other words, unconditional election promotes security. Conditional election promotes insecurity and restlessness. God's unconditional, electing love is the basis for the following famous text:

> For I am sure that neither death nor life, nor angels nor rulers, nor things present nor things to come, nor powers, nor

height nor depth, nor anything else in all creation, will be able
to separate us from the love of God in Christ Jesus our Lord.
(Rom. 8:38–39)

Now we see why, when Paul exults in God's manifold blessings,
he begins with election. "He chose us in him before the foundation of the world. . . . In love he predestined us for adoption as
sons" (Eph. 1:4–5).

Unconditional election is our security. Unconditional election is the key that helps us plumb the depths of God's glory.
Unconditional election is an exercise of God's free and unmerited grace, mercy, and love.

On the basis of the Father's election, the Son came to save
those whom he had chosen from before the foundation of the
world. In other words, election is the sure foundation of gospel
grace, of our conviction that God's love is unconditional.

PREACHING ELECTION TO YOURSELF

Those who regularly preach this truth to themselves are
encouraged. To Christians who are discouraged by their failings, to Christians who worry that their sins will separate them
from God's love, unconditional election says, "Because God did
not choose you on the basis of your performance, he will not
reject you for your failure to perform. You are secure. His love
is not conditioned on what you do. He chose you because he
delights in you. There is no other reason."

This teaching is not a license for sin. That is because the
first sign of new birth is a longing for holiness and a profound
desire to turn from sin. Christians are citizens of God's kingdom.
They delight in God's authority. In fact, an ongoing apathy about
obedience might be a sign that a professing Christian has not
experienced new birth.

To one who is discouraged by an unbelieving friend's
stubborn refusal to believe the gospel, election says, "Nothing

can keep God from saving. No one can resist God's will. God is sovereign. He is all-powerful. Keep praying. Keep witnessing. Don't give up. God can change even the most hardened heart."

To the person wondering how God could possibly love him, election says, "You will never know *why* he chose you and not another, but he did." Unconditional election is God saying, "I have loved you from before the foundation of the world, not on the basis of your performance, but despite its absence."

Those who know the joy of preaching the gospel to themselves don't stumble over unconditional election. Rather, like Paul, they lead with this wonderful truth:

> Blessed be the God and Father of our Lord Jesus Christ, who has blessed us in Christ with every spiritual blessing in the heavenly places, even as he *chose us in him* before the foundation of the world, that we should be holy and blameless before him. *In love he predestined us* for adoption as sons through Jesus Christ, according to the purpose of his will. (Eph. 1:3–5)

When we feel discouraged, guilty, or inadequate, the doctrine of election is a sure tonic. When we feel proud and tempted to look down on others, the doctrine of election is the humbling cure.

The first thing that should go through your mind when the alarm stirs you from slumber, and the last thing before your head hits the pillow, should be, "God, thank you for choosing me to be one of your children."

Here is an example of what it might look like to preach the Father's electing love to yourself.

> Father, thank you for choosing and electing me. Your choice was a decision of sovereign grace. For reasons that cannot be explained, you have delighted in me from eternity past. I did nothing to deserve it. You picked me and sent your Son to save me simply because you are love. There is no other reason.

Because your electing love is unconditional, I am eternally secure. I praise and worship you.

Discussion Questions

1. What was the main point of this chapter?

2. What was your favorite passage in this chapter? Why?

3. Read Ephesians 1:3–6 and Romans 9:6–21. What do these texts tell us about God's electing love?

4. What is the difference between conditional and unconditional election?

5. In your opinion, what is the biggest objection to unconditional election?

6. What benefits accrue to the person who learns to preach the doctrine of unconditional election to himself?

7. When do you preach the gospel to yourself?

Further Reading

- Grudem, Wayne. *Systematic Theology: An Introduction to Biblical Doctrine*. Grand Rapids: Zondervan, 1994. See esp. chaps. 16, "God's Providence," and 32, "Election and Reprobation."

- Pink, Arthur W. *The Sovereignty of God*. Blacksburg, VA: Wilder Publications, 2008.

- Sproul, R.C. *Chosen by God*. Wheaton, IL: Tyndale, 1986.

- Storms, Sam. *Chosen for Life: The Case for Divine Election*. Wheaton: IL, Crossway, 2007.

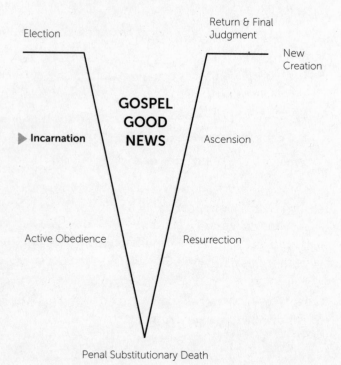

Election

Return & Final
Judgment

New
Creation

GOSPEL
GOOD
NEWS

▶ Incarnation

Ascension

Active Obedience

Resurrection

Penal Substitutionary Death

The Great Descent

Now that we are preaching God's election to ourselves, we can rest more secure in God's love. The doctrine of the incarnation, the next doctrine in the gospel sequence, will make God's astonishing love even more apparent.

I am in my mid sixties, but I still love to exercise. My weapon of choice is a thirty-year-old, eighteen-speed touring bicycle that I bought for $150 at a garage sale. Despite the price, it works great. A couple times a week I ride for exercise. I don't go very far, and I don't go very fast, but it is a great stress reliever, and it keeps my blood pressure down.

I don't have expensive bicycle clothing. When the weather is warm, I wear an old black swimming suit and a moisture-wicking T-shirt that I purchased at Walmart. My shoes are fifteen years old, my skin is pasty white, and I have way too much body fat (a reason for the exercise).

On a recent ride, God spoke to me powerfully. About three miles out, I got a flat tire. I dragged my bike into the ditch to repair the tire. (Did I mention that I am not very mechanical?) Fifteen minutes later, the repair was not progressing like the manual said.

Like a good Samaritan, another cyclist saw me in my predicament and graciously pulled over to help. He was about forty, pedaling a $5,000 carbon-fiber road bike. He was wearing a professional cycling outfit that probably cost $500. This man was sculpted. I don't think he had one percent body fat. His lightly bronzed skin covered muscles that bulged in all the right places.

He could see that I was in trouble. "Can I help?" he graciously asked.

"I am having trouble changing my tire."

From a hidden pocket he pulled out a set of expensive, ultra-light bike tools and quickly helped with the repair.

"How far are you riding today?" I asked.

"About sixty-five miles. I'm training for a two-hundred-mile race. How about you?"

Slightly embarrassed, I exaggerated, "About fifteen miles." I didn't volunteer that this was the longest ride I'd done in two months.

By this time, I—the fat grandpa on the thirty-year-old bike in a cheap outfit—was feeling thoroughly intimidated. I was embarrassed. I wanted him to think well of me, but there wasn't much about me to commend a high opinion.

I got back on my bike. My friend was soon just a blur on the horizon. I nursed my emotional wounds for a couple of miles. Just as I was starting to feel better, I saw two bicyclists way off in the distance. As I got closer, I got a better look. They were two overweight people on one-speed bikes, the kind with bulging, bouncy balloon tires, wobbling down the street at about five miles per hour. I quickly gained on them, and as I passed them I began to feel superior. *Look at those slow-moving, out-of-shape people. Isn't it wonderful that I am not like them; that I am in such good shape?*

About a mile later, the Holy Spirit's sweet conviction came. Pride is the great sin. Few know that as well as I do. I wrote the book *Gospel-Powered Humility* to make this point.[1] Pride is the sin that feeds all the others. It is at the heart of what made the Devil fall (Isa. 14:12–18). It is the root of Original Sin, and I had just witnessed two profound symptoms of that besetting sin in my own heart.

The first was the feeling of intimidation I felt when the fit, serious cyclist stopped to help me fix my flat. I felt intimidated in his presence because I wanted to be something that I wasn't. I wasn't a no-body-fat, sculpted guy with expensive equipment. I was just an overweight sixty-something out for some exercise. I wasn't happy with who I was, the stage of life I was in, or the body that God had given me. Humility would have contentedly thanked God for the way he had made me. It would have rejoiced in my friend's sculpted physique. But pride is never content with its situation. It always lusts for more. Humility would have thanked God for my weakness and my friend's strength. But that was not me. No, I desired to be something I wasn't. That was Satan's sin. "I will make myself like the Most High" (Isa. 14:14). My feeling of intimidation was a signpost pointing to the evidence of this terrible sin at work in my heart.

The second symptom was even worse. It was the condescending attitude that welled up in my heart as I passed the two overweight cyclists. Now the table had turned. I had the upper hand. I was actually looking down on other people who were in the same position I had been in a little while earlier. I looked down on them because I felt superior. It was ugly. It was sin. I was proud. I needed a Savior!

The good news is that the gospel gives me a Savior, so I paused and preached the good news of the incarnation to myself.

SALVATION NEEDED

Pride is a problem. We are born with Original Sin. Its source is Adam. Pride is the heart and soul of this sin. It affects us constantly, mostly in ways of which we are not aware.

The Serpent told Eve that when she ate of the forbidden fruit, she would "be like God, knowing good and evil" (Gen. 3:5). She couldn't resist the temptation, and so she ate. Then she convinced Adam to eat. Their eyes were opened—not to the reality that they were divine, but to the *deception* that they were something that they were not. They wanted to be divine. That was the problem. When they allowed that desire to blossom, God judged them. The deception that they were more than they were was God's judgment. In other words, God gave them up to that desire. From that day to this, the fundamental problem of the human family has been the lust for self-exaltation, coupled with a dissatisfaction with who and what we are. It dominates us from the moment of conception.

Pride, the corruption at the heart of Original Sin, is the evil that nourishes all the other sins. For example, we are impatient with others because we think our needs, ideas, or values are more important than theirs. In the same way, selfishness is an expression of pride. I act selfishly because I think I am more important than you. Therefore, it is my happiness at your expense. Another obvious expression of pride is boasting. How about critical speech? We criticize others because we feel superior, or because we really feel inferior and we want to make ourselves look better. The examples could go on and on.

Pride is also responsible for most of our pain, suffering, and sorrow. As we saw in my story, pride is the root of most insecurity, striving, restlessness, and unhappiness. "But what about those who are caught up in self-pity, who are self-absorbed with a sense of failure?" asks Stuart Scott. "This too is pride. They are just on the flip side of the pride 'coin.' People who are consumed with self-pity are focusing on their own selves too much."[2]

Here is the good news: Christ's incarnation saves proud people. It is an important aspect of the gospel. God provides it to atone for the arrogance of Christians like you and me.

AN INFINITE STEP DOWN

The term *incarnation* describes Christ's self-emptying. The Son of God lowered himself and took a human body. He shared two natures—divine and human. Even though he had two natures, he was only one indivisible person. This concept is utterly unique to Christianity.

The incarnation is not a doctrine that anyone would dream up. All the tendencies of our sinful nature run the other way— toward self-exaltation. When we invent gods, they are like us. That is why the gods of the ancient Greeks, Romans, and so on were selfish, self-exalting, and self-obsessed. The prose on an old Christmas card said it best: many men have claimed to be God, but only once has God descended to become man. Think of the Caesars, the Pharaohs, Maharishi Mahesh Yogi, and most New Age seers. They all seek divinity. But the incarnation turns all this on its head. God lowered himself, utterly emptied himself, and became man!

To appreciate this, we must think in terms of God's infinity. Infinity means that God has no boundaries, no limits, and no end point in any of his attributes. They go on forever. For example, because God is a spirit, he has no physical properties. A body would confine him and render him finite. "To say that God is infinite," wrote A. W. Tozer, "is to say that He is measureless."[3]

By definition, therefore, anything *finite*, no matter how big, when set next to something infinite, recedes, by comparison, into nothingness. If God is infinite, the universe itself, with its billions of stars and trillions of light years, is so small that it is almost irrelevant when set next to him. It is finite. As the infinite God gets larger and larger, compared to his finite universe, the universe gets comparably smaller and smaller. This is what Psalm 145 means when it says that God's "greatness is unsearchable" (v. 3). In the words of the prophet Isaiah,

> Behold, the nations are like a drop from a bucket,
>   and are accounted as the dust on the scales;
>   behold, he takes up the coastlands like fine dust.
> . . . .
> All the nations are as *nothing* before him,
>   they are accounted by him as *less than nothing* and
>   emptiness. (Isa. 40:15, 17)

The nations are a "drop from a bucket"! Think about it. That means that, compared to God, the seven billion people currently alive on earth are like only one little drop from a bucket that at one time held millions of drops.

Isaiah continues. The nations are only "fine dust" on God's scales. What does dust weigh? Essentially nothing. It is irrelevant. It cannot move the scales up or down. It is meaningless.

It gets worse. All the nations—past, present, and future—are "accounted by him as *less than nothing and emptiness*." How can anything be less than nothing and emptiness? Emptiness is a low point. But less than nothing is less than emptiness. This we cannot imagine.

But we are not emptiness. We are real flesh and blood, all seven billion of us. So why did Isaiah write this? He knows we are finite, and he knows that God is infinite. He also knows that anything finite is almost meaningless compared to something infinite.

I am writing this not to depress you—just the opposite. You need this information to appreciate the incarnation. To the degree that sin becomes bitter, grace will become sweet. To the degree that we see ourselves for who we really are, the incarnation will become utterly astounding. It is because we think so highly of ourselves that the incarnation has so little impact upon us.

If Jesus Christ is God, and if he descended from an infinitely glorious status to take to himself a finite human nature, then it follows that his descent was an *infinite* emptying. He traveled an *infinite* distance downward. This is the measure of God's love for small, insignificant, finite creatures like you and me. And it is because of this that Paul describes God's love in infinite terms. He calls it "*love . . . that surpasses knowledge*" (Eph. 3:19).

Here is how John Flavel, one of the great seventeenth-century Puritan preachers, grappled with this truth:

For the sun to fall from its sphere, and be degraded into a wandering atom; for an angel to be turned out of heaven, and be converted into a silly fly or worm, had been no such great abasement; for they were but creatures before, and so they would abide still, though in an inferior order or species of creatures. The distance betwixt the highest and lowest species of creatures is but a finite distance. The angel and the worm dwell not so far apart. But for the infinite glorious Creator of all things, to become a creature, is a mystery exceeding all human understanding. The distance between God and the highest order of creatures is an infinite distance.[4]

Why did Christ descend an infinite distance? He descended an infinite distance to atone for our sins—offenses that are infinitely serious in God's sight.

SEVEN STEPS DOWN

In the Bible, seven is the number of completion or perfection. In the second chapter of his letter to the Philippians, Paul describes the incarnation in terms of a sevenfold descent:

> Have this mind among yourselves, which is yours in Christ
>   Jesus, who, though he was in the form of God, did not
>   count equality with God a thing to be grasped,
> but emptied himself,
> by taking the form of a servant,
> being born in the likeness of men.
> And being found in human form, he humbled himself by
>   becoming obedient
> to the point of death,
> even death on a cross. (Phil. 2:5–8)

Did Not Grasp for Equality

First, verse 6 tells us that although Jesus was equal with God, he did not grasp for that equality. "Grasping" for equality with others is our knee-jerk reaction to almost every situation. That is how I related to the fit cyclist who helped with my flat tire. In my heart, I grasped for equality. I lusted for his approval and acceptance. In fact, pride goes so deep in us that we are seldom content to grasp for equality. Instead, we ultimately grasp for superiority.

But Jesus did the opposite. He "did not count equality with God a thing to be grasped." As we contemplate this, it is important to remember that he was not a junior God. He was not inferior to his Father. Although he was God the Son, he was completely equal in power, might, and majesty with God the Father. He was fully God!

Despite this, the text tells us that he "did not count equality with God a thing to be grasped." Instead, he opened his hand and let go of his right to divine glory. To a rights-infatuated culture, this is a foreign concept. Jesus emptied himself of his right to the perks of divinity. He joyfully placed himself under his Father's authority and submitted unquestioningly to his every command. This is the attitude that must be present before anyone will submit to authority. It is the attitude of wives, children, citizens, and employees who submit to human authority. Even though equal in value, they do not grasp for equality with those around them. They relinquish that right. They make the wishes, needs, wants, and success of those around them more important than their own.

Emptied Himself

Jesus also took a second step down. Verse 7 tells us that he "emptied Himself." The idea is that of turning a bucket upside down and completely pouring out its contents. Of what did he empty himself? He didn't empty himself of his divinity. As we have seen, Jesus was fully God. He could never quit being divine.

He emptied himself of the benefits and rewards of divinity. So, for example, in his humanity he emptied himself of omnipotence (all power) and strengthened himself with weakness

(2 Cor. 13:4). He emptied himself of divine omniscience, which is absolute knowledge. When asked about the timing of his second coming, he responded, "Concerning that day and hour no one knows, not even the angels of heaven, *nor the Son*, but the Father only" (Matt. 24:36).

He emptied himself of immortality. He voluntarily submitted to death. He emptied himself of the right to ceaseless angelic praise, and became an object of shame and ridicule. He emptied himself of the right to judge. Instead, Jewish and Roman courts judged him. This is just a fraction of what the Bible means when it says that he emptied himself.

Slavery

Verse 7 tells us that he took a third step down. He became the Father's slave, "taking the form of a servant." The word translated "servant" by the ESV is the Greek word *doulos*, the word for a common slave.

Our culture despises slavery. We remember slavery in the Old South before the Civil War, and we are repulsed by the very thought. However, Jesus became a slave. He surrendered the right to make his own decisions. He became utterly dependent. "The Son can do nothing of his own accord," Jesus said, "but only what he sees the Father doing" (John 5:19). And that was not a burden. Rather, Jesus was delighted to have it this way. "My food is to do the will of him who sent me and to accomplish his work" (John 4:34).

Became Human

Then Jesus took a fourth step down. Verse 7 tells us that he was "born in the likeness of men." The Creator of all things took a part of his creation, a human body, to himself. "In the creation," wrote Thomas Watson (1620–1686), "man was made in God's image; in the incarnation God was made in man's image."[5] This was no small humbling.

God is infinite. He is so far beyond his creation that the second commandment forbids worshipping him with or by any material image, picture, or object. Yet Christ condescended to take to himself a finite human body—not temporarily, but *forever.* This should never cease to astound us.

Obedience

Fifth, Jesus humbled himself with obedience. Like slavery, obedience is an unpopular idea in the Western world. Our culture values freedom, autonomy, and self-fulfillment. But Jesus' obedience was an expression of voluntary slavery. Just as disobedience is an expression of pride, willing obedience is an expression of humility. Obedience says to the person you are obeying, "You and your ideas are more important than me and my ideas right now."

Obedience is always ultimately to God, not to men. We obey human authority because we want to please God. This was Jesus' posture. His obedience was first to his equal, God the Father. To please God the Father, he obeyed his parents, the local rabbi, and even the tyrannical ruler, Pontius Pilate. This did not demean Jesus. Just the opposite! It empowered him. It delighted him. "I delight to do your will, O my God; your law is within my heart" (Ps. 40:8). "My food is to do the will of him who sent me" (John 4:34).

Death

Sixth, Jesus "humbled himself by becoming obedient to the point of death." God the Father asked him to die. Because Jesus had taken the posture of a slave, he unhesitatingly said, "I delight to do your will" (Ps. 40:8).

"What's the big deal?" you ask. "Doesn't everybody die?"

We die because we are sinners. "In the day that you eat of it you shall surely die," God warned Adam (Gen. 2:17). "The wages of sin is death" (Rom. 6:23). However, Jesus was (and is)

42

the *sinless* Son of God. Because he had never sinned, he was immortal. But for this act of obedience to his Father, he would never have died. In addition, the Bible tells us that death is God's implacable enemy (1 Cor. 15:26). God hates it. It reminds him of sin, judgment, and human failure.

Jesus would have remained immortal. He never would have died, unless he somehow took our sin upon himself. This he agreed to do in the garden of Gethsemane. The next day, with our sin imputed to him, he went to the cross and died a criminal's death. He submitted to, even immersed himself in, the very thing he hated most—death!

That is incomprehensible humility.

Death on a Cross

Last, Jesus didn't just die. He submitted to the most horrible form of capital punishment ever invented by humans. He submitted to death on a cross. When we say something is *excruciating*, we are unknowingly referencing the cross. In the middle of *excruciating* is the Latin word for the cross, *crux*. Something excruciating is terribly painful and very hard to bear. It is something as nasty as the cross.

Jesus' seven steps down were an infinite humbling. As we have noted, the distance between something infinite and something finite is by definition infinite. It is immeasurable. Jesus' status, glory, and majesty were and are infinite. He left all this to enter our finite world. It was an infinite condescension.

So far, this chapter has said that we need a great salvation, one that will atone for the pride that saturates every cell of our being. I made it my ambition to be equal to or better than the fit cyclist who came to my rescue. Then I looked down on the slow, overweight cyclists. The incarnation was the exact opposite. God's Son made it his ambition to travel an infinite distance down. He became a man. Jesus descended into almost nothingness in order to make God the Father, and you and me, more important than himself.

SO WHAT?

This book is about preaching a wide-angle gospel to ourselves. The incarnation is the crucial second event in that gospel. It expresses a pride-conquering humility, and it lays bare the heart of the divine nature.

We don't think much about pride. We are much more concerned about adultery, murder, and drug addiction. But, to God, pride is the big sin. It motivates adultery, murder, and drug addiction. The incarnation convinces us that this is true. The Bible constantly repeats this unchanging principle. He who exalts himself will be humbled, but he who humbles himself will be exalted. All disobedience to God expresses pride, just as all obedience expresses humility. This means we have all exalted ourselves. God is infinitely just, and his justice demands that we be humbled into hell forever.

But there is good news! When people believe the gospel, their faith unites them with Christ in his life, death, and resurrection. This means that their faith unites them with Christ in his incarnation. As we have seen, Jesus' incarnation was an infinite step down. This was necessary because our sinful pride is against an infinitely holy God. Therefore, it is infinitely serious. As a result, an infinite descent by Jesus was necessary to atone for my infinitely serious pride.

When we believe the gospel, Christ's willingness to forego his equality with his Father becomes ours, his self-emptying becomes ours, his perfect slavery to the Father becomes ours, and his obedience unto death, even death on a cross, becomes ours. In short, his humiliation becomes ours.

Now the principle, "He who humbles himself will be exalted," works in our favor. Because Jesus went so low, God raised him to the highest place (Phil. 2:9–11). Because our faith unites us with Christ, his humiliation becomes ours, and his exaltation also becomes ours. In other words, Christ's incarnation was part of the suffering that he voluntarily undertook to atone for our arrogance. He took the humiliation that proud, rebellious sinners deserve, so that we could get the exaltation that he deserves. This is a source of great joy and gladness for proud sinners who believe the gospel.

To the despairing, this means hope and joy.

To those who feel the sting of their personal arrogance, this means liberation from guilt and condemnation.

To the selfish, the incarnation offers solace and encouragement. Even though we are proud, when God looks at us he sees the humility of Christ. On that basis, he must exalt us. He must receive us into heaven forever. This sounds as if he is reluctant. He is not. Rather, it is with exalted joy that the Father will welcome us. Christ's incarnation has conquered our ugly arrogance and pride.

Those who believe this, and turn from their sin, refuse to listen to self. When they talk too much at a party, they don't entertain voices of condemnation. When they boast inappropriately, they don't listen to the words of self-hating accusation that come the next morning. When they spend thirty minutes talking about self and later feel the sting of conviction, they don't beat up on themselves. Instead, they repent. Then they preach the incarnation to themselves repeatedly. Here is an example of what that might look like.

> Father, I am an arrogant, self-centered sinner. I deserve to be humbled forever in hell. But the measure of your love for me is this. Your Son made an infinite descent. He did this to atone for my pride, which is infinitely serious in your sight. You have imputed Christ's humility to me. Someday I will be exalted on the basis of that humility. Oh Father, thank you, thank you, thank you. I am and will be forever and eternally grateful for your Son's incarnation and my participation in it through faith.

Discussion Questions

1. What was the main point of this chapter?

2. What was your favorite passage in this chapter? Why?

3. What are some symptoms of pride in your own life?

4. What did Jesus do to solve your pride problem?

5. Which of Jesus' seven steps down was most relevant to you? Why?

6. What would it look like for you to preach the incarnation to yourself?

Further Reading

- Grudem, Wayne. *Systematic Theology: An Introduction to Biblical Doctrine.* Grand Rapids: Zondervan, 1994. See esp. chap. 26, "The Person of Christ."

- Packer, J. I. *Knowing God.* London: Hodder & Stoughton, 1973. See esp. chap. 5, "God Incarnate."

- Watson, Thomas. *A Body of Divinity.* 1692. Reprint, Edinburgh, UK: Banner of Truth, 1958. See esp. part IV, chap. 6, "Christ's Humiliation in His Incarnation."

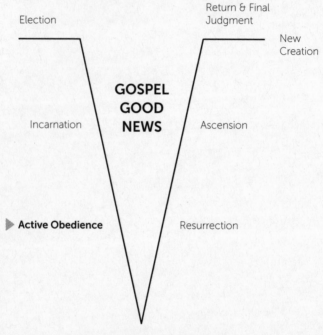

Election

Return & Final
Judgment

New
Creation

GOSPEL
GOOD
NEWS

Incarnation

Ascension

Active Obedience

Resurrection

Penal Substitutionary Death

4

No Hope without It!

The standard for entrance into God's kingdom is perfection! Sadly, many Christians are unaware of this. They think their best effort will be enough. They reason that God grades on the curve. But nothing could be further from the truth. "You therefore must be perfect," Jesus said, "as your heavenly Father is perfect" (Matt. 5:48).[1]

If this is true, then everyone is in trouble, especially those who are most religious, for they are most apt to rely upon their own virtues in order to gain God's acceptance.

J. Gresham Machen (1881–1937), one of the twentieth century's Christian heroes, understood God's standard. Most would consider him a good man, certainly much better than most, but he rejected dependence upon his virtues to gain God's acceptance.

He was a professor of New Testament at Princeton from 1918 to 1926. But eventually he took a courageous stand against the modernism that infiltrated Princeton after World War I. That stand proved costly, and he was forced to leave. He founded Westminster Theological Seminary in Philadelphia, funding a large share of its start-up costs from his personal inheritance. When the Presbyterian Church in the USA later rejected him, he founded the Orthodox Presbyterian Church. He was a man of principle, solid piety, and great theological knowledge. Many consider him one of the twentieth century's outstanding Christian leaders.

On a speaking trip to North Dakota in the winter of 1936–1937, he contracted pneumonia. As he lay dying in a remote Midwestern hospital, he sent this telegram to his friend, John Murray: "I am so thankful for the active obedience of Christ. No hope without it."

The next day he died, secure in God's acceptance.

ACTIVE OBEDIENCE DEFINED

What is the active obedience of Christ? Why would Machen write Murray that he had "no hope without it"? Why would its absence cause hopelessness?

The answer is the subject of this chapter. We are thinking about a big-picture gospel and how to preach it to ourselves. So far, we have examined God's electing love and the incarnation. The active obedience of Christ is the third aspect of the gospel that we need to preach to ourselves every day. It solves our need for perfection.

When people believe the gospel, their faith unites them to Christ. In God's eyes, they become all that Christ is and was. In the last chapter, we learned that this allows us to share both in Christ's humiliation and in his exaltation.

This chapter goes further. Here is how Paul puts it: "For our sake he made him to be sin who knew no sin, so that in him we might become *the righteousness of God*" (2 Cor. 5:21).[2] What is the righteousness of God? It is God's moral perfection. It is the "perfection" that Jesus tells us we must have before we can enter God's kingdom (Matt. 5:48). "As it applies to man," note Bridges and Bevington, the righteousness of God "refers to the righteousness that God *requires* from man, a righteousness no sinner can provide on his or her own."[3] Christ becomes, amongst other things, our "righteousness" (1 Cor. 1:30). In other words, righteousness is the moral "perfection" that Christ requires from us.

The active obedience of Christ is his life of sinless perfection, his righteousness, imputed to the Christian. He is the only person who ever earned God's favor by performing or working. Christ is the only perfectly righteous person who has ever lived.

OUR GREAT NEED

I have a great need for Christ's righteousness. I am not perfect. I am a flawed human being, who nevertheless believes the gospel. In the last twenty-four hours, I have been irritable with my wife (a symptom of pride). I have complained about my health (a symptom of coveting). I have grumbled about America's political situation (another symptom of pride). I have had to restrain the temptation to be impatient with others (selfishness). Most importantly, for hours I have thought about everything except God (idolatry). Maybe you are like me.

Some would say, "What's the big deal? No one is perfect. Aren't you a bit introspective? God knows our frame. He knows we are imperfect, and he loves us anyway. So lighten up!"

Here is the biblical response: Sin is serious. The unbeliever faces God's wrath (Rom. 1:18). Why? The standard is perfection. We are imperfect, and nothing can remove God's anger but perfection—what the Bible calls "the righteousness of God" (Rom. 3:21–26).

If this is true, as we have already noted, attempting to merit God's acceptance by trying harder or being more sincere is a waste of time. The only way one can get perfection is through the imputation of Christ's righteousness—what Machen called his active obedience. Theologians call this an alien righteousness. By "alien" they mean it is not something we produce. It comes from outside of us. Christ earned it, and he freely, graciously, and joyfully gives it to those who believe the gospel.

To one who understands his or her problem, the imputation of the active obedience of Christ is the best news anyone could possibly hear. To understand the nature of this marvelous gift, we need to say more about God's law, which expresses his righteousness, and how Christ fulfilled it.

THE IMMUTABLE LAW

First of all, God's law is immutable. That means it never changes. It is never put aside. It is never done away with. God's law is an expression of his unchanging righteousness. As such, it does not go away. On the day of judgment, you and I will be measured by our obedience to God's law.

That is not the way many Christians understand it. They think that somehow the New Testament set aside God's law, that God is no longer interested in his law, or that it is no longer the standard by which God will measure us. Nothing could be further from the truth.

Martin Luther (1483–1546) initiated the Protestant Reformation. He understood the importance of God's law. Before his conversion, Luther was a member of an order of monks called the Augustinian Hermits. They were renown for their asceticism, for their daily punishment of their bodies in their attempts to merit salvation. Luther knew that God's law was unchanging, and that God required righteousness. He probably didn't understand righteousness as perfection, but he knew that God's requirements would never go away. Therefore, he was terrified. He lived in constant guilt and anxiety. He knew he didn't measure up.

His confessor was a monk named Father Staupitz, and Luther drove Staupitz crazy. Luther would confess every little sin, sometimes for hours. Then he would leave, remember a sin that he had forgotten, and hurry back to confess more.

In order to relieve Luther's scruples, Staupitz sent him away to study for a doctorate in theology. When Luther finished his studies, he began to give lectures to the other monks, first on the Psalms and then on Romans. It was at this time that he came to Romans 1:16–17.

For I am not ashamed of the gospel, for it is the power of God for salvation to everyone who believes, to the Jew first and also to the Greek. For in it the *righteousness* of God is revealed from faith for faith, as it is written, "The *righteous* shall live by faith."

Luther was stumped by the expression "the righteousness of God." What did Paul mean? Was the righteousness of God a quality in God, or was it something that God required of believers? Luther was determined to find out. He pounded on this passage, wrestling day and night with God. Finally it came to him. Through the gospel, to all who believe, God gives the righteousness that Luther so painfully lacked. It was that simple. Righteousness was God's free gift to all who trust in Christ. "Thereupon I felt myself reborn," he said, "and to have gone through open doors into paradise."[4]

This is what Luther discovered: God did not take away the Old Testament law. He satisfied it. God did not relax his standard of perfection. Rather, his Son fulfilled it. The law did not go away. On the day of judgment, God will still measure all men by his law. But here is the good news: Jesus obeyed God's law perfectly. When we believe the gospel, God unites us with Christ in such a way that his obedience is imputed to us. Now, on the basis of Christ's performance, not our own, God considers us to have satisfied his law. In other words, God gives us the gift of Christ's righteousness, and the gift does not wax or wane with our performance. It is no wonder that Luther thought he had "gone through open doors into paradise."

What we are saying is that Christ's active obedience satisfies the immutable law of God. Practically, what does that look like?

JESUS OBEYED GOD'S LAW

Jesus' obedience was a Trinitarian work. Because the Father is love, he sent his Son to obey his law on our behalf. As we saw in the last chapter, because Jesus is also love, he agreed to come, and for him that meant an *infinite* condescension. Because the

Holy Spirit is love, he came to motivate and empower Jesus to obey God's law. The three persons of the Trinity cooperated to accomplish all of this. Let's think about some of God's requirements and how Jesus satisfied them.

The Bible tells us that it is our duty to do everything for the glory of God (1 Cor. 10:31). However, in our fallen world, lesser motives usually energize us. In fact, we do many things for the glory of self, not of God. We boast about our accomplishments. We talk about ourselves too much. When we see a family picture, our first concern is to find ourselves in it and see how we look. We drop the names of important people we know at the office water cooler. What is the solution?

Jesus lived his whole life for the glory of God. He had no other motive. For example, knowing he would face the supreme test of the cross on the following day, and highly tempted to give in to lesser motives, Jesus prayed, "Now is my soul troubled. And what shall I say? 'Father, save me from this hour'? But for this purpose I have come to this hour. *Father, glorify your name*" (John 12:27–28). When we believe the gospel, God imputes Christ's passion for God's glory to us. His active obedience becomes ours.

How about the Ten Commandments? Jesus obeyed the first commandment. He never put a strange God before him. Nothing ever mattered more than the Father and his will. How about the third commandment? He never used God's name in vain. How about the fourth? The Pharisees accused Jesus of breaking the Sabbath, but actually he was the only person who perfectly fulfilled the Sabbath. Jesus also obeyed the fifth commandment: honor your father and mother (Luke 2:51). He never transgressed the commandment against adultery. He never looked at a woman lustfully. Speaking of Christ, Psalm 40:8 sums up his heart-attitude. "I delight to do your will, O my God; your law is within my heart."

Two great commandments sum up God's law. The first is, "You shall love the Lord your God with all your heart and with all your soul and with all your mind and with all your strength" (Mark 12:30). No one reading this has done this for more than a few minutes, and that very infrequently, but Jesus did it waking and sleeping, around the clock. "I always do what pleases him" (John 8:29 NIV). "My food is to do the will of him who sent me" (John 4:34). Here is the good news. When we believe, God imputes Christ's keeping of the Ten Commandments to us. He also imputes Christ's perfect love for his Father to us. His active obedience becomes ours.

Jesus also perfectly fulfilled the second great commandment, "You shall love your neighbor as yourself" (Mark 12:31). God's love is more than a feeling of affection. It is the willingness to pursue the happiness of another, even at great personal expense. Jesus' death modeled what this looks like. That is how we want others to love us. The "expense" to Christ was *infinite*. It was slow, tortured death by crucifixion, and here is the astounding truth: Jesus did this for his enemies, not his friends.

Another biblical commandment is that we love God more than people, even family members. Again, Jesus comes to the rescue. He prioritized the family of God over his biological family. One day he was teaching a large group. His family members arrived, demanding special attention. But Jesus responded, "Whoever does the will of God, he is my brother and sister and mother" (Mark 3:35).

We could go on and on. Jesus is our forgiveness. He forgave lavishly. He is our love for enemies. He died for his enemies. He is our sexual purity. He loved both the opposite sex and his own sex properly. He is our contentment. He never coveted. He is our faith. He trusted God perfectly. All of this is what Paul had in mind when he wrote to the Corinthians, "And because of [God] you are in Christ Jesus, who became to us wisdom from God, *righteousness* and sanctification and redemption, so that, as it is written, "Let the one who boasts, boast in the Lord" (1 Cor. 1:30–31).

This is what Jesus meant when he said, "Do not think that I have come to abolish the Law or the Prophets; I have not come to abolish them but to *fulfill* them" (Matt. 5:17). Jesus did not save us by abolishing the law. He saved us by fulfilling it. The term that describes that work of fulfillment is Christ's active obedience.

FREED BY CHRIST'S ACTIVE OBEDIENCE

So what does this mean for us as Christians? It means amazing liberty. It is what Paul meant when he said, "For freedom Christ has set us free" (Gal. 5:1). Under the old covenant, a believer had to earn righteousness through personal effort. God gave the law to the Jews to convince them that this was an impossible task (Rom. 3:20; 5:20; 7:13). Therefore, the Old Testament saints received salvation, just as we do, by putting their trust in the Messiah to come. Our union with Christ in his active obedience means that the demands of God's law have been satisfied by him on our behalf.

This does not mean that we are free to live lawlessly. Rather, it means that our best efforts are now adequate. It means that we can fail, and because of Christ's active obedience, we are always and eternally acceptable to God the Father. Because Jesus obeyed the law perfectly, we don't have to do so in order to be saved.

Because Christ obeyed the Old Testament dietary laws, we are free to eat anything. Because Christ fulfilled and obeyed all the Old Testament laws about feasts and feast days, God considers us to have fulfilled them, and now every day is equally holy.

So what is our responsibility? Are we free to live according to the whims and passions of our selfish desires? No! Paul sums up God's simple requirements in Galatians 5:6 with the words "faith working through love." In other words, believe the gospel and express that faith by sacrificially loving God and man.

SO WHAT?

First, and most importantly, because this is true, there is absolutely no ground for boasting in our good works or sincere efforts. Rather, "Let the one who boasts, boast in the Lord" (1 Cor. 1:31). This means that we are not significantly better than those around us. When tempted to look down on someone else, we need to preach the truth of this chapter to ourselves. It might go something like this:

> Father, the standard is perfection. I am a million miles away from this. I live by faith in Christ's righteousness imputed to me. I have no saving virtues in which to boast. I am deeply humbled by the gospel. I am a fellow sinner, a beggar pleading for grace, just like this person I am tempted to look down on.

Here is how Paul said it in Galatians 6:14. "Far be it from me to boast except in the cross of our Lord Jesus Christ, by which the world has been crucified to me, and I to the world."

There is a second application, and it brings us the most glorious freedom. My wife and I got into an extended fight over a petty issue. All the while, I bounced back and forth between blaming her and blaming myself. Despite all of this, I was able to rejoice in the active obedience of Christ. No matter who was at fault, my standing with God was untouched. I was covered by the active obedience of Christ.

You are still clothed in the active obedience of Christ even when you fail to love others properly, which happens daily. Give up on perfection. You can't produce it. Seek godliness with all your heart, but rest in the truth that, because of Christ's active obedience, God will accept your best efforts even though they are imperfect. Most Christians waste a lot of time beating themselves up because they don't meet their own standards, let alone God's. Those who understand God's standard, and his provision, give up on themselves. They enter into a profound spiritual rest.

God's rest is not a lack of activity. It is not a lack of obedience. Just the opposite. God's rest motivates increased activity.

When you feel condemned for impatient words spoken thoughtlessly to a loved one, there is rest in the active obedience of Christ. It clings to those who cling to the gospel.

For the third time, a friend shared the gospel with his unbelieving father. When his father didn't seem to understand what he was talking about, my friend became impatient with him. This turned his father off and shut down their communication. A few months later, his father died without believing the gospel. My friend was devastated. He felt tremendous guilt for his impatience and lack of love. He felt responsible for his father's failure to respond.

When he came to me for counsel, I said, "On a human level, you might be responsible for his unbelief. Yes, you probably blew it, but it is OK."

"How can it be OK?"

"None of us is perfect. In fact, we can't even get close to perfection. The good news is that God has clothed you in Christ's active obedience. Jesus never blew an evangelistic opportunity. Because you believe the gospel, in God's sight, his obedience, patience, and perfect wisdom have been credited to your account."

My friend left rejoicing. How about you? Are you living in the joy that belongs to those who preach the imputation of Christ's active obedience to themselves?

It is no wonder that Gresham Machen telegraphed John Murray from his deathbed, "I am so thankful for the active obedience of Christ. No hope without it." Everyone who understands God's requirements, human sinfulness, the judgment to come, and the free imputation of Christ's righteousness feels the same way.

So what would it look like to preach the active obedience of Christ to oneself? Here is an example.

Father, I am a great sinner. I am utterly incapable of satisfying the demands of your law. But you are a great lover. You sent your

Son to do what I cannot do. You sent him to fulfill the demands of your law. My faith in the gospel has united me with your Son. It has imputed his active obedience to me. I am now free from the law's demands. To relate to you, I don't need to be perfect. Why? All my failings—past, present, and future—are buried out of sight under the active obedience of Christ.

Hallelujah!

Discussion Questions

1. What was the main point of this chapter?

2. What was your favorite passage or paragraph in it?

3. Why did J. Gresham Machen exult in the active obedience of Christ as he lay dying?

4. What did you learn about God's law?

5. What lies do you speak to yourself (and listen to) on a daily basis?

6. What truth does God want you to preach to yourself?

Further Reading

- Bridges, Jerry, and Bob Bevington. *The Great Exchange: My Sin for His Righteousness.* Wheaton, IL: Crossway, 2007.

- Grudem, Wayne. *Systematic Theology: An Introduction to Biblical Doctrine.* Grand Rapids: Zondervan, 1994. See esp. chaps. 36, "Justification (Right Legal Standing Before God)," and 42, "Glorification (Receiving a Resurrection Body)."

- Piper, John. *Counted Righteous in Christ: Should We Abandon the Imputation of Christ's Righteousness?* Wheaton, IL: Crossway, 2002.

- Sproul, R. C. *Faith Alone: The Evangelical Doctrine of Justification.* Grand Rapids: Baker, 1995.

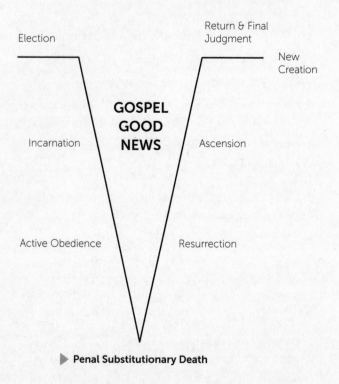

5

The Heart of the Matter

This book is about preaching to yourself rather than listening to yourself. So far we have studied election (chapter 2), the incarnation (chapter 3), and the active obedience of Christ (chapter 4)—all important subjects to preach to oneself on a daily basis. This chapter is about the fourth event in the gospel sequence, the atonement—and it has a strong connection with chapter 4.

Jesus' death on a Roman cross was the culmination of his active obedience.

JARED'S GUILT

Like many Christians, Jared struggled with guilt.[1] "Before I was a Christian, I entered into a sexual relationship with a married woman," he told me. "She became pregnant. I put tremendous pressure on her to get an abortion. She was an evangelical. She was convinced that abortion was wrong. So at first she resisted. However, after prolonged and aggressive intimidation, she finally submitted."

"What did her husband say?" I asked.

"He never knew. He was out of town with the military for a year."

Jared paused for a moment, and then he continued. "Six months ago, I became a Christian. Since my conversion I have begun to understand just how evil my actions were. The feelings of guilt have only grown stronger with time. I know I am supposed to walk in God's forgiveness, but I still feel guilty. I can't help it."

"Do you believe that God loves you?"

"I know that the Bible says he loves me, but I seldom feel it. Furthermore, others around me seem to feel his love. When I don't, it makes me wonder if I am really a Christian."

"When you think about God, what comes to mind?" I asked. "What is God like?"

"Many confusing thoughts," he answered. "Sometimes I think that God is kindly and good. At other times, I am afraid of him. I want to believe that God is good. I know the Bible says he is, but I am not always sure."

Jared struggled with two problems that are common to many Christians. First, unresolved guilt oppressed him, and, second, he seldom felt God's love. He was good at listening to himself, but not good at preaching to himself. Learning to preach the cross of Christ to oneself solves these two problems. Let's take them one at a time.

GUILT IS UNIVERSAL

First, Jared's unresolved guilt. A mother of two once told me, "I carry so much guilt that I have stretch marks." What she meant was that she carried the weight of her guilt like a pregnant woman carries her child. So great was the stress that it left stretch marks on her psyche. Her words describe the daily experience of many, including my friend Jared. Physical stretch marks from pregnancy often remain for life. Without Christ's atoning work for our guilt, the stretch marks it leaves on our conscience will never really leave, either. The gospel is a message of good news. It is the solution for Jared's guilt and ours, and it leaves no stretch marks.

Guilt is a universal human experience. It occurs when we contradict our consciences by something we do or fail to do. When we feel guilty, we feel responsible. We feel shame. We feel that we deserve punishment. Conscience will continue to hound us until punishment occurs or our guilt is somehow removed.

A Roman Catholic friend struggled with guilt. Every night before bed, he removed his shirt and beat his back with a small whip. Sometimes it drew blood. He was trying to expunge his guilt with self-atonement. We Protestants can do the same thing, but our punishment differs. We might hate ourselves for three or four days until our self-hatred finally makes us feel like we have atoned for our sin. The means are different, but the end is the same. We are attempting to quiet the voice of conscience by self-atonement.

The feeling of guilt can range from a minor irritation to a crushing sense of failure that is utterly immobilizing. Sometimes the feeling persists for days, months, or even years. In severe cases, shingles, diarrhea, hives, or insomnia are the side effects. Guilt can be utterly shattering. With some, like Jared, it can linger for years. We can feel guilty about sins we have committed against ourselves, other individuals, society at large, or God himself.

In addition, guilt can be false. We can feel guilty for things that are morally neutral—for example, drinking a beer or failing to recycle.

Guilt can also go on vacation. If we work hard enough at suppressing it, we can silence the accusations of conscience. Western culture has effectively done this with such sexual sins as fornication and homosexuality.

Ultimately, however, our feelings have little to do with it. Whether we feel guilty or not, when we break God's law, we are in fact guilty, and we will give an accounting to God for those thoughts or actions on the day of judgment.

God sent his Son to solve our guilt problem. He did this by fully punishing our sins, removing them far from his sight (Ps. 103:12). On the day of judgment, the sins of those who have believed the gospel will not be remembered.

SIN PUNISHED

Our sins will not be remembered because two wonderful things happen when we believe the gospel. First, God imputes Christ's active obedience to us. We discussed this in the last chapter. Second, God imputes all our sins to Christ. He gets the punishment that our sins deserve. We call the combination of these two truths the doctrine of double imputation. Christ imputes his righteousness to us, and our sins get imputed to Christ.

Christ's punishment is the measure of sin's seriousness. Because Jesus bore my sin, God, using the Romans, strung Jesus out on a cross and tortured him to death for six hours. God poured out his wrath on his Son in my place and yours. Since Christ is God, he has an infinite capacity for suffering. For this reason, he was able to fully atone for even the most heinous sins, sins such as Jared's adultery and murder.

We tend to salve our guilt by minimizing the severity of our sin. But God doesn't do it that way. Instead, he maximizes the seriousness of our sin. He puts Jesus on the cross and says, "This is how serious your sin is. It deserves crucifixion. And this is also how extravagant my love is. Now rest in my forgiveness. Rest in my love." When Jared encouraged his lover's abortion, he was encouraging murder. The penalty for murder in the Old Testament was death by stoning. Here is the measure of God's love. Through his death on the cross, Jesus bore the death penalty that Jared deserved. Anyone in Jared's position who stares straight into this truth, and fully embraces it, will find tremendous freedom. He will also gain a deep sense of the wonder of God's love. This is how God dissolves guilt. He makes sin more serious in order to make his love more amazing, and ultimately this causes us to surrender our efforts at self-atonement.

There is now no need for Jared to hate himself, condemn himself, or try to atone for his sins through self-punishment.

We tend to feel guilty until our sin has been punished, and God looks at our sin in the same way. He has not winked at Jared's sins. He has not minimized them. Rather, at the cross our sins were completely and thoroughly punished. God exhausted his wrath on his Son in Jared's place.

This is why, as we have already seen, Paul describes God's love with the language of infinitude. His love "surpasses knowledge" (Eph. 3:19).

SIN REMOVED

In addition, God has removed our sins far away from himself. *Expiation* is the word that describes this process. It means that he has covered them or removed them from his sight. This includes Jared's sin of adultery and his conspiracy to murder his unborn child. In the words of Psalm 103:12, he has removed our sins from us "as far as the east is from the west." That is an immense distance.

I live close to the Hanford Nuclear Reservation in central Washington. Since World War II, the plutonium for most of our nuclear bombs has been produced there. As I write, there are about 208 million liters of nuclear waste decaying in underground tanks at Hanford. This waste is lethal. Anyone directly exposed to it will die within a few days. It will not be safe for thousands of years. Therefore, it must be removed far from the public and kept out of contact for ages.

In the same way, our sin must be removed from God's sight. To God, sin is like radioactive material. He is too pure even to look at evil (Hab. 1:13). Because our sin has tainted the creation, even the moon and stars are impure to him (Job 25:4–6). Someday they will flee from his presence (Rev. 20:11). It will be the same for those who do not believe the gospel (Rev. 6:15–17). Therefore, sin must be removed from both our sight and God's.

Long before the nuclear age, God gave us a beautiful picture of this in the sixteenth chapter of Leviticus. Once each year, on the Day of Atonement, the high priest entered the Most Holy Place to atone for the sins of Israel. At God's command, the high priest presented two goats. The first was slaughtered. Its blood was brought into the Most Holy Place and sprinkled on the mercy seat. It atoned for the sins of the people.

The second was the scapegoat. The high priest, representing all of God's people, laid his hands on the scapegoat. This act symbolized the transfer of Israel's sins to the animal. The goat was then led far away into the wilderness, never to be seen again. In other words, the sins of God's people were transferred to the goat and "removed" from the sight of God and his people forever.

This is what Jesus did for Jared and every Christian reading these words. Jesus became our scapegoat.

Think back on Christ's trial. After listening to the accusations against Jesus made by the Jews, Pilate turned to the Jewish people and said, "I find no guilt in this man" (Luke 23:4). Pilate was stating the obvious. Jesus was the only guiltless man who has ever lived. Despite his innocence, all of our guilt and sins were transferred to him. Then he went to the cross and took the punishment that both we and our sins deserve. He died, and when he died our sins died with him. Like Hanford's nuclear waste, they were buried with Christ in a rich man's grave. They were removed from God's sight and from ours.

I explained the atonement and the scapegoat to Jared. As I did, his load seemed to lighten, his countenance changed, and hope rose in his eyes. I exhorted him to preach these truths to himself. I encouraged him to do this every time the feelings of guilt returned until the reality of God's love conquered the guilt and sorrow.

FEELING GOD'S LOVE

We began by stating that Jared had two problems—unresolved guilt and the inability to feel God's love. We have seen how the cross helped Jared with unresolved guilt. This brings us to the love of God. The cross does more than settle the issue of guilt. It proclaims God's love for guilty sinners. So how could I help Jared to grow in his capacity to feel God's love?

God's love is not primarily a feeling. It is a passionate desire for our happiness, even at great personal expense. Jesus didn't just talk about the love of God. He demonstrated it. The title of Gary Chapman's book, *Love Is a Verb*, says it all. God's love is focused on doing, not feeling. *Love* is an action word. God expressed his love at Calvary. As we have noted, it is a love that "surpasses knowledge" (Eph. 3:19). Why would Paul say that?

God's love is a holy love. The opposite of holiness is commonness. To be unholy is not necessarily to be sinful. It is to be common. It is to be like the world we live in. Therefore, to be holy is to be set apart from the world, to be different, to transcend the world, its values, and its customs.

The way that God's love is holy, or different—the way that it "surpasses knowledge"—is this: God loves his enemies. When we were his enemies, Christ died for us (Rom. 5:8, 10). The people of this world love only their friends, those who treat them well. Both non-Christians and many Christians refuse to love their enemies. However, when Jesus died for us, he died for his enemies. He gave his life for his enemies. Another way to say this is that he gave his life for those facing his wrath (Rom. 1:18). God's love is the happiness of his enemies at his expense. This means we can understand God's love only to the degree that we feel our sin—that is, the depth of our enmity toward God in our pre-Christian state.

Although we have said that God's love is not primarily affection, affection is important. It is a fruit, or consequence, of God's love. God sent his Son to die for us in order to remove the enmity that separates us. He did this because God wants to be our Friend. He wants to feel affection for us.

So, in summary, God's love is holy because it is an action, not a feeling—a benevolent action performed for enemies.

Second, God's love is holy because God, the Lover, is not compelled by anything outside of himself. We have already noted that the only thing God owes us is justice. Most people assume that they are basically good and that God owes them a reward. Then they are offended when he doesn't give it to them. But God owes us only justice. Despite this, the Father commanded his Son to come and save us by giving himself to be tortured to death on a Roman cross. God was not duty-bound to love us. His love was free. It was not coerced by a debt he owed us. It was given voluntarily.

So, in summary, here is the love of God. Jesus Christ gave himself to be slowly tortured to death on a cross. He did this not for his friends, but for his enemies. He did this to make his enemies his friends. Nothing compelled him. He owed us nothing but justice. Yet, despite this, he suffered infinite pains to extend amazing grace to us. God's love is a passionate desire for our happiness. It is our happiness at his expense. He incurred the expense in order to feel and express affection for us.

I explained all this to Jared. Then I reminded him of God's command in Jude 21, "Keep yourselves in the love of God."

"How do I do that?" Jared asked.

Here is how I responded. First, Jude wants you to preach these truths to yourself. Speak these truths to yourself day and night. It has nothing to do with how you feel. Feelings come and go, but God's love is a constant reality. Ultraviolet light surrounds us continually. You can't see it, but that doesn't mean it isn't there. How I feel about it is irrelevant. In the same way, no matter how we feel about God's love, it is always there.

I encouraged Jared to fill his mind with these truths, and told him that the more he did so, the more he would *feel* God's love. Meditating on the love of God is a daily discipline that all growing Christians practice.

Here is an example of what it might look like to preach God's love to myself. "God loves me. How do I know? Look what he did for me. It matters little how I feel. God has declared his love with action." It is either true or it is not. There is no middle ground. Nothing can separate a true believer from God's love (Rom. 8:39), not even the believer's sins and failings.

SO WHAT?

Why does all this matter? First, it matters because our love for God and others is always a response to God's love for us. "We love because he first loved us" (1 John 4:19). In other words, to the degree that I internalize and deeply understand God's personal love for me, I will want to love God and man as God has loved me. It will affect whom I love and how I love them.

For example, Jesus commanded us to love our friends, but he also commanded us to love our enemies (Matt. 5:44). Why? Because when we were his enemies, God loved us. This is an example of what Jesus meant when he commanded us to be holy, as he is holy (1 Peter 1:15–16). Our love is to be like God's love.

God's love is also the basis for my willingness to forgive those who have hurt me. Jesus told us to forgive seventy times seven times (Matt. 18:21–22). Why? The Father forgave us an infinite debt. Our forgiveness was infinitely costly to the Father and the Son. If this is true, how can I accept God's forgiveness and not forgive others? My sins are infinitely serious in God's sight. No one can sin against me infinitely. No matter how deeply they hurt or wound me, their offense can never be infinitely offensive to me.

In addition, God's love for us provokes love for God in return. That was Jared's experience. As he thought about the enormity of his sin, and how Jesus took the death penalty he deserved, he was overwhelmed with God's personal love for him. He gradually became an extravagant server and lover of God. Jared's life became God's glory at his expense.

My explanations didn't instantly remove Jared's feelings of guilt and his inability to feel God's love, but as he preached these truths to himself rather than listening to himself, his life began to change. His meditations on the cross slowly drove his guilt away. The more he preached the love of God revealed in the cross of Christ to himself, the more he felt it. Then, as he sensed God's love for himself, he began to extend that love to those around him. He began to love the unlovable. He became a lavish forgiver. He began to serve others as Christ had served him.

Here is an example of how Jared preached the cross to himself.

> Father, thank you for sending your Son to forgive an unworthy sinner. Thank you for loving me with an infinite love. Jesus took the punishment that my sins deserve, so that I could receive the eternal reward that his virtues deserve. Thank you for removing my sins from your sight. Thank you for loving me with deeds, not just words. Thank you for the atoning death of Jesus Christ, which makes an affectionate relationship between us possible. Thank you for acting to secure my forgiveness.

Discussion Questions

1. In your own words, sum up the content of this chapter.

2. What was your favorite quote or paragraph? Why?

3. Do you struggle with guilt? If so, with respect to what?

4. How should you apply the atonement to your guilt?

5. When are you unable to feel or relate to God's personal love?

6. How has this chapter altered your view of God's love?

7. What do you say when you preach the reality of the atonement to yourself?

Further Reading

- Farley, William P. *Outrageous Mercy: Rediscovering the Radical Nature of the Cross.* Phillipsburg, NJ: P&R, 2009.

- Mahaney, C. J. *The Cross Centered Life: Keeping the Gospel the Main Thing.* Colorado Springs: Multnomah, 2002.

- Stott, John R. W. *The Cross of Christ.* Downers Grove, IL: InterVarsity Press, 1986.

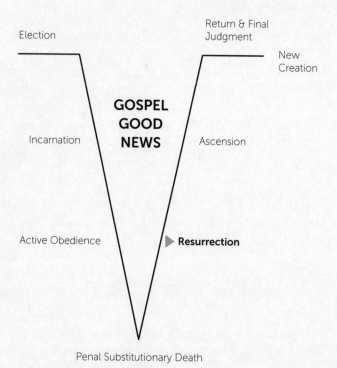

6

Hope for the Hopeless

The resurrection is the next aspect of the gospel to preach to ourselves. To appreciate Christ's resurrection, however, we first need to think hard about death.

Death is ugly. It is unpleasant. A few years ago, I went to the hospital to visit a man who had only a few days to live—an old friend who I had known in better times. He was dying of a disease that affects the nervous system. Sadly, I arrived too late to pay my last respects. He had just entered a coma from which he would not recover.

I will never forget the scene. He was thin and emaciated. He had lost a hundred pounds. His skin was yellow and flaky. Although he was in a coma, his eyes and mouth were open, as if mocking his unconscious condition. He drooled uncontrollably. His browning eyes testified to the gradual shutting down of his liver. He breathed with loud raspy sounds; each breath was an effort. His frame was stiff and rigid. The room smelled of death.

Ours is a culture of youth and life. We will do almost anything to avoid thinking about scenes like this. We rush corpses to the mortuary so that no one will see them. We marginalize our stooping, wrinkled elderly to long-term care facilities. For many, the elderly are social lepers, and we pretend that it will never happen to us—but it will. There are only two options: premature death or the ravages of old age. Neither is pleasant.

How does the non-Christian cope with all this? Normally he just accepts death. He has no other option. He has no concept of resurrection. To him, death is just part of living. Francis Bacon (1561–1626), the father of the scientific method, wrote, "It is as natural to die as to be born."[1] We take the same attitude when we say, "In this world, nothing is certain but death and taxes."

But Christians should never think like this. According to the Bible, death is an aberration. It is not part of God's original plan. It is a blight on creation. It is a perversion of the intended order. It is God's just judgment for sin. This is the Christian worldview. Christians see death differently. They despise it, because it reminds them of the horrors of sin. It says, "Sin is horrible. Look at what it does to us. Sin is awful. Look at how much God hates it."

This chapter is about better news. Christ's resurrection has conquered death. It began what Peter called the "restoration of all things" (Acts 3:21 NKJV). That includes the restoration of immortality. Growing Christians do not listen to their nagging fears about death. They preach the resurrection to themselves.

Paul was convinced that Christ's resurrection was "according to the Scriptures." He wrote,

> For I delivered to you as of first importance what I also received: that Christ died for our sins in accordance with the Scriptures, that he was buried, that he was raised on the third day *in accordance with the Scriptures.* (1 Cor. 15:3–4)

By "the Scriptures" he meant the Old Testament. Those were the only Scriptures Paul had. This chapter will survey the subject of resurrection from Genesis to Revelation. We will then pause to discuss the experience of resurrection. Our main point is simple: Christ's resurrection conquered death. We will examine death and resurrection from three angles— creation, fall, and redemption.

CREATION

God created men and women in his image and likeness (Gen. 1:26–28). God is immortal. We can speculate that a large reason for Adam's immortality was that he shared God's image and likeness.

The first indication that death was even a remote possibility came with God's warning to Adam. "You may surely eat of every tree of the garden, but of the tree of the knowledge of good and evil you shall not eat, for in the day that you eat of it you shall surely die" (Gen. 2:16–17). The threat of death implied the absence of death at the time of the threat. But Adam's immortality and God's warning were not the end of the story.

FALL

We all know the story. Adam and Eve sinned. It wasn't one of the big sins—incest, adultery, murder, drug addiction, or alcoholism. No, it was just a little sin, stealing some forbidden fruit. However, this one little sin brought death to Adam, to Eve, to the cosmos, and to every person descended from them. This is the measure of sin in God's sight.

First came spiritual death. Sin unplugged Adam and Eve from God, the source of all spiritual and physical life. Spiritual death eventually produced physical death. Like a battery exhausting its charge, their bodies slowly wound down. Nine hundred years later, they died (see Gen. 5:3–5). In addition, it wasn't just Adam. God subjected the entire cosmos to the curse of death.

> For the creation was subjected to futility, not willingly, but because of him who subjected it, in hope that the creation itself will be set free from its bondage to corruption and obtain the freedom of the glory of the children of God. (Rom. 8:20–21)

Because God is merciful and gracious, he immediately announced a rescue plan: "I will put enmity between you and the woman, and between your offspring and her offspring; he shall bruise your head, and you shall bruise his heel" (Gen. 3:15).[2] Although Genesis 3:15 says nothing about death, the reversal of the curse implied the restoration of immortality.

From this point forward, death is God's enemy. Because it reminds him of sin, judgment, and the obstruction of his plan, he opposes it. This is why, in the Old Testament, contact with a corpse made an Israelite ceremonially unclean (see Num. 19:11–19; 31:19–20).

REDEMPTION

Since death was not God's original plan, but rather a temporary exception to his plan, and in fact his enemy, Scripture began to prophesy a day of resurrection. Job clung to the hope of a future resurrection:

> For I know that my Redeemer lives,
>   and at the last he will stand upon the earth.
> And after my skin has been thus destroyed,
>   *yet in my flesh I shall see God,*
> whom I shall see for myself,
>   and my eyes shall behold, and not another.
>   (Job 19:25–27)

In the tenth century BC, King David announced his confidence in the resurrection: "My flesh also dwells secure. For you will not abandon my soul to Sheol, or let your holy one see corruption" (Ps. 16:9–10).

In the eighth century BC, Isaiah expanded David's hope. "And he will swallow up on this mountain the covering that is cast over all peoples, the veil that is spread over all nations. *He will swallow up death forever*" (Isa. 25:7–8). A few paragraphs later, Isaiah added, "*Your dead shall live; their bodies shall rise.* You who dwell in the dust, awake and sing for joy! For your dew is a dew of light, and the earth will give birth to the dead" (Isa. 26:19).

As the prophetic period was drawing to a close, Daniel took up the hope of future resurrection: "And many of *those who sleep in the dust of the earth shall awake,* some to everlasting life, and some to shame and everlasting contempt" (Dan. 12:2).

To confirm these important prophesies, there were three resurrections in the Old Testament. They occurred during the ministry of Elijah and Elisha. In 1 Kings 17, Elijah raised the son of the widow of Zarephath. Elisha had a double portion of Elijah's power. Therefore, there were two resurrections in his ministry. In 2 Kings 4, he raised a Shunammite's son. In 2 Kings 13, a corpse rose to life when it touched Elisha's grave.

By the time we get to the New Testament, resurrection momentum has been building for centuries. The expectation is strong, and God the Father is ready to move. Jesus came as the agent of resurrection life. "I am the resurrection and the life," he said (John 11:25). He predicted his own resurrection three times (Matt. 16:21; 17:22–23; 20:19). Here is an example: "From that time Jesus began to show his disciples that he must go to Jerusalem and suffer many things from the elders and chief priests and scribes, and be killed, and on the third day be raised" (Matt. 16:21).

In addition, as in the Old Testament, to encourage our hope in these prophecies, Jesus raised three people—the son of a widow in Nain, Jairus's daughter, and Lazarus.[3]

Jesus' resurrection was the culmination. It was the seventh in the Bible, and it differed from those that preceded it in three important ways. First, the previous resurrections concerned only the individuals involved. God raised them on behalf of no one but themselves. But Jesus' resurrection was corporate: God raised him as the representative of every person who would believe the gospel. When Jesus rose, all believers rose with him. This includes everyone in the Old Testament who put their faith in the Messiah. The first sign of participation in

Christ's resurrection is the restoration of spiritual life through the miracle of new birth. New birth is a spiritual resurrection.

Second, the six resurrections prior to Christ were temporary. Each resurrected person later died. But Jesus' resurrection was permanent. He rose, never to die again.

Finally, everyone prior to Christ was raised by someone else's power. But Jesus raised himself by his own power. "I lay down my life that I may take it up again. No one takes it from me, but I lay it down of my own accord. I have authority to lay it down, and I have authority to take it up again" (John 10:17–18).

THE DEATH OF DEATH

Christ's death also played an important part in our resurrection. We sum it up by saying, "Jesus died that we might live." Here is what that means.

We begin with two propositions. First, God is infinitely and absolutely just. Second, the penalty for sin is death. We are sinners. We deserve to die. This means that God must execute justice. He cannot give us immortality until the death penalty has been measured out to us.

That is one important reason that Jesus went to the cross. In our place, as our substitute, he died the death that we deserve. When we believe the gospel, God unites us with him in his death. His death becomes ours. Because God's justice has now been satisfied, we are now free to be united with Christ in his resurrection.

Here again is the amazing love of God. Jesus died the death that we deserve in order to unite us in the resurrection that he deserves.

ALREADY, BUT NOT YET

Why do we still experience physical death if we have been united with Christ in his resurrection? The answer is that the experience of Christ's resurrection is "already, but not yet." In other words, we Christians have begun to experience some of the benefits of Christ's resurrection. But the full gift will not be unwrapped until the last day. On that day, God will raise our bodies from the dust and reconstitute them. We will share his glory. God will clothe us with immortality. From that point forward, we will be unable to die.

What does it mean to experience the "already" of the resurrection? Our first experience of resurrection life comes to us through new birth, when God's Spirit indwells us. Spiritually, we move from death to life. God's Spirit gives us a small foretaste of the resurrection life to come. Here is what that life looks like.

First, God's Spirit gives us the gift of faith. He infuses us with a growing "conviction" and "assurance" that what God promises will really happen (Heb. 11:1).

Second, God's Spirit gives us new desires. We experience them as a growing yearning to obey God's word, take the low road, become small, and pour out our lives in service to God and man. This is what Peter means when he talks about our sharing the divine nature (1 Peter 1:4).

Third, God's Spirit gives us a growing conviction that Christ is infinitely good and glorious. He couples this with a growing hunger to "know" God the Father through his Son, Jesus Christ. The Holy Spirit comes to convince us that all of our happiness is tied up in knowing God the Father through God the Son by the power of God the Holy Spirit. This is a fundamental work of the Holy Spirit.

Fourth, the Holy Spirit gives some Christians a taste of the powers of the age to come. This happens, for example, when God supernaturally heals someone of a disease. The powers of the future have broken into the present. We should pray for this and expect it.

That is the "already." What about the "not yet" of the resurrection? The "not yet" of the resurrection is physical immortality—new bodies freed from disease, death, and decay.

What will our new bodies be like? Our best guess is that they will appear somewhat normal. Jesus arose with a resurrection body. He appeared to the disciples off and on for forty days. During that time, they recognized him. They touched him. They watched him eat food.

In addition, in 1 Corinthians 15:42–44, Paul gives us several facts about our resurrection bodies. First, he tells us that our new bodies will be raised imperishable. In other words, they will be unable to die or decay. In addition, he tells us that they will be raised in glory. This means that we will share the glory of Christ in our bodies. Then he tells us that they will be raised in power. They will be not weak, but powerful in a way that we cannot now imagine. Last, he tells us that they will be raised as "spiritual" bodies—that is, connected to both the spiritual and the physical worlds in ways that we do not now experience. These are general descriptions. We long for more specifics. What does Paul mean by "power"? What does he mean by "spiritual" bodies? We don't know, but someday we will.

Finally, the "not yet" should be a matter of great sobriety. Jesus warned us that all will be raised, both believer and unbeliever: "For an hour is coming when all who are in the tombs will hear his voice and come out, those who have done good to the resurrection of life, and those who have done evil to the resurrection of judgment" (John 5:28–29).

What makes hell so horrible is that it is experienced in the body. The torments are physical as well as social, mental, and spiritual. And what makes heaven so wonderful is that it is also experienced in the body. The pleasures and joys are physical as well as social, mental, and spiritual.

According to Hebrews, true faith is the "*assurance* of things hoped for, the *conviction* of things not seen" (Heb. 11:1). It is a growing confidence that all these things are true. It is the conviction that because I believe the gospel, I will participate in Christ's resurrection and all that it implies.

HOPE

Belief in the resurrection is the grounds for our hope, and hope motivates perseverance. One of the pastors who I work with said recently, "For believers, this life is as bad as it is ever going to get, but for unbelievers, this life is as good as it is ever going to get." That is the nature of our hope. This is as bad as it is going to get. Life will be nothing but better from this point forward.

Hope matters. At some point in life, we will experience problems like depression, financial shortage, sickness, old age, cancer, relational conflict, persecution, or Alzheimer's disease. Some couples are barren. Others have children who die young. One of my grandsons was born without an anus. Another developed a brain tumor in his preschool years. One of my granddaughters contracted the RSV virus a few days after birth and almost died. A friend just had life-altering surgery in her early twenties. In the prime of his life, my brother died of brain cancer. Another friend just experienced incredibly painful kidney stones. We live in a fallen world.

When these things happen, our self will preach, and it is fatal to listen. Those who persevere because they are growing in hope talk back to themselves. They preach the resurrection. Many reading these words need this hope right now. Others will need it later.

As we have seen, our hope is already here, but not yet here. We have begun to experience it, but not as clearly as we would like. I often rise in the dark. Then, when the first sliver of light begins to creep across the eastern sky, my hope rises. Day is coming. In the same way, Christ's resurrection is the first light of a new creation. It portends great things to come. The world still lies in darkness, but an all-conquering spiritual light is increasingly flooding the horizon of a new day to come. Do you see it that way?

PREACH TO YOURSELF

How should we respond? When trouble comes, don't listen to yourself. The self will look at circumstances and preach despair, hopelessness, and discouragement. Instead, talk back to yourself. Preach the hope of the resurrection.

Death is ugly and unpleasant, but the truth of Christ's resurrection is beautiful and encouraging. It dilutes the horror of death. It removes its sting.

The resurrection will terminate in the condemnation of unbelievers, but it will also terminate in the justification of believers. Do you preach this to yourself? Do you remind yourself of these things? Is this motivating within you a holy fear of God and a desire to share the gospel with the lost?

Just as death confronts us in the third chapter of the Bible, the promise of eternal life closes the second to the last chapter of the Bible. Rejoice in these amazing words: "He will wipe away every tear from their eyes, *and death shall be no more*, neither shall there be mourning nor crying nor pain anymore, for the former things have passed away" (Rev. 21:4).

Here is an example of what it might look like to preach this truth to yourself:

> Father, death is your just judgment for our sin. Today it is our normal experience. But you have promised something better, the resurrection of the dead. Death was never your plan. It is a distortion, an aberration of your holy purposes. That is why you sent your Son. He died the death that I deserve, so that I could rise with him in the resurrection that he deserves. Through the miracle of new birth, you have made this real to me. I hope for the life of the world to come, where there will be no more mourning, crying, or pain—a world where death has been swallowed up by your victory.

Discussion Questions

1. In your own words, what is the main point of this chapter?
2. Share with the group your favorite quote or paragraph.
3. What troubles, fears, or maladies have you experienced, for which hope in Christ's resurrection is a cure?

4. What is the connection between the resurrection and your new birth?

5. What future hope does the resurrection guarantee all believers? Which aspect of this future is most relevant to you? Why?

Further Reading

- Gaffin, Richard B., Jr. *Resurrection and Redemption: A Study in Paul's Soteriology.* 2nd ed. Phillipsburg, NJ: P&R, 1987.

- Grudem, Wayne. *Systematic Theology: An Introduction to Biblical Doctrine.* Grand Rapids: Zondervan, 1994. See esp. chaps. 28, "Resurrection and Ascension," 42, "Glorification (Receiving a Resurrection Body)," and 57, "The New Heavens and New Earth."

- Warnock, Adrian. *Raised with Christ: How the Resurrection Changes Everything.* Wheaton, IL: Crossway, 2010.

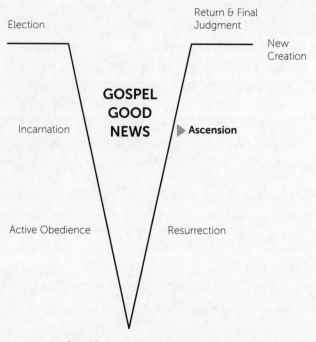

Election

Return & Final
Judgment

New
Creation

GOSPEL
GOOD
NEWS

Incarnation

Ascension

Active Obedience

Resurrection

Penal Substitutionary Death

The Forgotten Doctrine

The future of nations and cultures often turns on single, unnoticed details, quickly forgotten, which in retrospect prove decisive. Such was the papal election of 1550. It was one of the great turning points of church history and therefore of world history.

In his book *The Reformation*, Diarmaid MacCulloch tells the story of how an English cardinal was almost elected pope.[1] Thirty-three years after the beginning of the Reformation, the battle over biblical authority and interpretation had split medieval Europe into Protestant and Catholic camps. However, many Roman Catholic bishops and cardinals sympathized with the Reformers regarding the authority of the Bible and the crucial disputed doctrine, justification by faith alone. In addition, they wanted to heal the schism with the Lutherans. One of these men was Cardinal Reginald Pole (1500–1558).

Pole was a wealthy, aristocratic Englishman who had fled to Italy to escape persecution from his relative, King Henry VIII. Known for his piety, his desire to reform the church, and his deep sincerity, he was respected by all. In 1537, Pope Paul III elevated him to cardinal. As such, Pole attended the Council of Trent as one of the pope's three delegates. However, when the Council pronounced its anathema against justification by faith alone, Pole walked out and never returned.

As Pope Paul III lay dying, he asked the College of Cardinals to elect Pole as his replacement. In the first vote, Pole fell four votes short of the two-thirds required. After the second ballot, Pole was only one vote short, but that was as close as he would get. With each subsequent ballot, the English cardinal lost ground. Finally the College of Cardinals elected Julius III, a civil servant, to replace Paul III. They came within one vote of electing an English pope who was sympathetic to the Reformers. Had Pole been elected, who knows how church history would have changed? Having rejected Pole's possibly conciliatory leadership, the Catholic Church hardened its position, following the excesses of the Council of Trent.

Why did God allow this? Was God asleep? Did he not care? Did he lack authority to change things? The doctrine of the ascension speaks to these doubts and more.

We have discussed election, the incarnation, Christ's active obedience, his substitutionary death, and his resurrection. The ascension is the next doctrine in the gospel lineup. It convinces us that God cares a lot, and that there are no coincidences in life.

THE OVERLOOKED DOCTRINE

The doctrine of the ascension is indispensable. Without the ascension of Christ, there would be no salvation. Without it, there would be no hope for the future. That is, there would be no assurance that God controls our lives and our futures. Without the ascension, history would be capricious and meaningless.

Despite this, the ascension is one of the least discussed and least celebrated gospel events. We make much of the incarnation at Christmas and the resurrection at Easter, but the ascension is largely ignored. Augustine (354–430), one of history's most influential thinkers, wrote that Ascension Day "confirms the grace of all the festivals together [Christmas and Easter], without which the profitableness of every festival would have perished. For unless the Saviour had ascended into heaven, his Nativity would have come to nothing ... and his Passion would have borne no fruit for us, and his most holy Resurrection would have been useless.'"[2]

We need to heed Augustine, for the importance of the ascension is often overlooked, even though its impact on everyday life is momentous. The ascension matters for at least five reasons:

- It is essential to our salvation.
- It is the precondition for the gift of the Holy Spirit.
- It means that Jesus continuously intercedes for us.
- It means that God hears our prayers.
- It assures us that Christ is in control of every detail in history. There are no accidents.

Let's examine these five points one at a time.

Ascended to Save

The first reason that the ascension matters is that it was necessary to complete our salvation. Although Christ lived, died, and arose while on earth, that work was not finished until he ascended and sprinkled his shed blood on the mercy seat in the heavenly tabernacle (Heb. 9:11–14).

The tabernacle of ultimate importance is the one in heaven. Moses' tabernacle was a replica of one that God showed him in heaven (Heb. 8:5). In addition, Jesus is the High Priest who serves the heavenly tabernacle. The Levitical high priests entered the Holy of Holies in the earthly tabernacle once a year to sprinkle the blood of sacrificial animals on the mercy seat. By doing so, they secured God's forgiveness for unintentional sins committed during the previous year. This rite needed to be repeated on the Day of Atonement each year.

All of this found fulfillment in Christ. Ultimately, he was the High Priest to whom the Old Testament priests pointed. He ascended into heaven with his own blood, sprinkled it on the mercy seat in the heavenly tabernacle, and thereby secured for

all time forgiveness for all our sins—past, present, and future
(Heb. 9:11–10:18).

To guilty, insecure Christians, this is tremendous news.
They no longer listen to their failures, inadequacies, and idio-
syncrasies. Instead, whenever sin (past, present, or future)
causes them to feel discouraged or defeated, they preach the
ascension to themselves.

Precondition for the Holy Spirit

We don't receive the gift of the Holy Spirit because we have
earned it. We receive the gift of the Holy Spirit because Jesus
earned it. God exalted Jesus to his right hand and, on the basis
of his sinless life and atonement, gave him the gift of the Holy
Spirit (Acts 2:33). In fact, it was the outpouring of the Holy Spirit
on Pentecost that confirmed Christ's ascension to the Father's
right hand to receive the title Lord and Christ (Acts 2:33–36).

The ascension was a necessary precondition for our recep-
tion of the Holy Spirit as an indwelling, life-giving presence.

Ascended to Intercede

The third reason that Jesus' ascension matters is that Jesus
ascended to intercede for the saints. After Jesus sprinkled his
blood on the mercy seat, he sat down at the right hand of God
to intercede for his church, day and night. He continuously
and eternally intercedes for each saint by name. And since he
is one with the Father, all his prayers are answered. This truth
has several wonderful applications.

First, it means that Christ is always *for us*. He is never
against us. In the back of their minds, many Christians imagine
that Jesus' intercession goes something like this: "Father, judge
[insert your name]. Punish him for his weaknesses and failings.
I am upset. Deal with him." But that is never the case. Jesus is
always "for" those who put their faith in him. He is never against
them. "If God is *for* us," asked Paul, "who can be against us?"

(Rom. 8:31). The question is rhetorical. It implies the answer. God is never against us. He is always for those who believe the gospel. He is always on our side. He is always rooting for us.

Some of you are thinking, "Yes, but you don't know what I have done or failed to do." You are right. I don't! But I don't need to know. God's Word is clear. Christ's active obedience (chapter 4) and his substitutionary death (chapter 5) are adequate for the worst sins imaginable. No sinner is beyond the reach of God's mercy. If God has atoned for your sin, then you are his friend, on his team, no matter how you feel. This means that Christ is always interceding "for you"!

His intercession is an expression of his love. Sometimes I feel depressed. When I do, it is often because I am listening to my feelings. But when I stop and preach the ascension to myself, I am reminded that Jesus is right now at the right hand of God, interceding for me. He is for me. He is not against me. Every detail of my life, even this depression, has been ordered by his intercession. It is his special gift. Immediately my mood changes. My spirit soars. As I contemplate Christ's ascension and what it means for me practically, the joy of the Lord burns away the fog of depression.

Christ's intercession also puts a dent in condemnation. "Who is to condemn?" asks the apostle Paul. "Christ Jesus is the one who died—more than that, who was raised—who is at the right hand of God, *who indeed is interceding for us*" (Rom. 8:34). Do you get the drift of Paul's logic? The one who loved you so much that he gave himself up to a brutal death is the same intercessor who is at God's right hand pleading for you. He didn't ascend into heaven to condemn you. Christ cannot condemn you and intercede for you at the same time.

In addition, we should note that Christ is not necessarily praying that you and I will have an easy life. Sometimes he prays for painful circumstances. Why? Because he loves us. He disciplines the sons whom he loves. He disciplines us to expand our capacity for future glory. "For this light momentary affliction is preparing for us an eternal weight of glory beyond all comparison" (2 Cor. 4:17). Notice: the afflictions are light and momentary, but the glory is weighty and eternal. The more you exercise a muscle, the larger it gets. The more you stretch a balloon, the larger its capacity becomes. The more a Christian suffers with his eyes on Christ, the more God expands his capacity for future glory.

God has given Christ the necessary authority to bring his intercessory work to pass. The one who intercedes for us is sovereign over all events, past and future (Matt. 28:18). All his intercessory prayers are answered. This means there are no haphazard events in our lives.

Grounds for Our Intercession

The fourth reason that Christ's ascension matters is that it is the grounds for our intercessory prayers. These chapters have stressed our union with Christ. That union has even now seated us with Christ in the heavenly places (Eph. 2:6). That is our position when we come before the Father in prayer. United with Christ, we are now clothed in his active obedience. All our sins are completely atoned for. As we learned two chapters back, they have been expiated. Now the Father delights in our intercession, just as he delights in his Son's.

Ascended to Rule

The fifth reason that the ascension matters is that Jesus ascended to rule. What makes Christ's intercession so potent is that the Father gave him dominion, lordship, and sovereignty over all affairs on earth. To understand why this is important, we need to think back on God's purpose for man's creation. One of the purposes for Adam's creation was to exercise God's rule on earth. "And God said to them, 'Be fruitful and multiply and fill the earth and subdue it and have *dominion* over the fish of the sea and over the birds of the heavens and over every living thing that moves on the earth'" (Gen. 1:28).

When we hear the word *dominion*, we often think of tyranny, oppression, or the selfish use of others for personal gain. But this was not God's plan. He created people to exercise *servant*-dominion. They were to rule by serving, bringing happiness to others at their own expense.

When Adam and Eve sinned, they forfeited the right to rule. As we have seen, people now use their power to enrich and empower themselves at others' expense.

However, Adam's failure did not cause God to give up on his plan to rule the earth through a servant-ruler. In the fullness of time, God sent a second Adam. Born to a virgin in a lowly stable, Jesus was Israel's long-awaited Messiah. As the "son of David," he came to fulfill God's promise that one of David's descendants would sit on God's throne. As the "second Adam," he came to establish the servant-dominion that God created the first Adam to exercise. As the "Son of God," he came to return the rule of God to earth.

Jesus became the servant-ruler that God created Adam to be. He did the utterly unexpected. At the time, no one understood it. He died to enrich the subjects of his kingdom. As we saw in chapter 3, he "emptied" himself to advance the happiness of his subjects at his own expense. In other words, the cross was the son of David's throne. From that throne, he showed us what Adam's rule was to look like. This is utterly counterintuitive to our fallen minds.

The Messiah's descent also meant a transfer of authority. God has sown an immutable principle into creation. He who humbles himself will be exalted, and he who exalts himself will be humbled. As we saw in chapter 3, Jesus' incarnation and death constituted the greatest humbling in history. "Therefore," exulted Paul,

> God has highly exalted him and bestowed on him the name that
> is above every name, so that at the name of Jesus every knee
> should bow, in heaven and on earth and under the earth, and
> every tongue confess that Jesus Christ is Lord, to the glory of
> God the Father. (Phil. 2:9–11)

In other words, the dominion that God created the first Adam
to exercise, the second Adam now possesses, and he possesses it because of his infinite descent.

This is good news! It means that the one who intercedes
for us is sovereign. He has the power to bring to pass all his
requests. This means that nothing in time and space is an
accident. The vote in the College of Cardinals that failed to
elect Reginald Pole was no accident. It happened that way
because Christ was interceding. When a child contracts
cancer, it is no accident. Christ brings all things to pass
through his high priestly intercessory work. And he means
it all for the ultimate good of his saints. When the stock
market collapses, it is no accident. Should World War III
start tomorrow, it will be no accident.

Some would answer that God is too good to bring painful events to pass. But that flies in the face of Scripture.
Remember, the Devil had to get God's permission to afflict
Job (Job 1:6–12), and Job didn't blame his suffering on the
Devil. Instead, he said, "The Lord gave, and the Lord *has
taken away*" (Job 1:21). Then he asks, "Shall we receive good
from God, and shall we not receive evil?" (Job 2:10). Jeremiah
adds, "Is it not from the mouth of the Most High that good
and bad come?" (Lam. 3:38). And the prophet Amos writes,
"Does disaster come to a city, unless the Lord has done it?
(Amos 3:6). "I form light and create darkness," wrote Isaiah.
"I make well-being and create *calamity*, I am the Lord who
does all these things" (Isa. 45:7). Yet the opposite is also true.
God never tempts us or incites us to evil (James 1:13–15).

SO WHAT?

Brothers and sisters, the implications of the ascension are life changing. It is on the basis of Christ's dominion and intercession that Paul pens these famous words: "For those who love God all things work together for good" (Rom. 8:28). When I found out that my grandson had brain cancer, Christ's ascension emboldened me to pray, "Father, it is OK. Christ has ascended. He is on the throne of history. William's cancer has happened *because* Christ is interceding for me, my wife, my son, my daughter-in-law, and my grandson. You are for us. I know that you are not against us. Because I believe that Christ has all authority and power, I know that this is no accident. Whether my grandson lives or dies, you mean it all for good."

In addition, because of the ascension, life and history have meaning. As I write these words, our culture is changing. People are anxious. Some are fearful. What does the future hold? But Christ's ascension proclaims the truth that history is going somewhere. It is purposeful. There are no accidents. A good and holy Savior is in control, and he is working all things according to the counsel of his will. After the Democratic party won a local election, a friend who understands this well said, "I voted for the Republican, but God voted for the Democrat."

In the end, Christ will subdue all his enemies. The second Adam is doing what the first Adam failed to do. He is exercising God's dominion on earth. The cross is the signature of that authority. Christ is a servant-ruler.

Confidence in the ascension has motivated great missionary activity. Because men like William Carey (1761–1834), the father of the modern missionary movement, believed in the ascended Christ, they traversed oceans and endangered their families, confident that the ascended Christ, sovereign over all things, would use their meager efforts for his glory.

This was Stephen's experience. As the Jews began to stone him, he looked up and saw Jesus standing at the right hand of

God (Acts 7:55–56). Greatly encouraged, he forgave his enemies and died in the comfort of the Holy Spirit, knowing that King Jesus had ordered his death and was using it for good.

Last, the ascension also means that the one who is our King and Lord is also our great High Priest. He is not a despot. The one who rules is also the one who ascended into heaven to sprinkle his blood on the heavenly mercy seat. The one who intercedes is continually for us. In the words of the *Tyndale Bible Dictionary*,

> The Ascension means that there is a human being in heaven who sympathizes with humanity and can therefore intercede on humanity's behalf (1 Jn. 2:1). Jesus has experienced everything that we have experienced—birth, growth, hunger, fatigue, temptation, suffering, and death—and therefore he can serve effectively as an intermediary before God in heaven (Heb. 2:17; 5:7–10). Christ's ascension assures the church that God understands the human situation and that Christians can therefore approach him boldly with their own prayers (Heb. 4:14–16).[3]

CONCLUSION

Preach to yourself. Don't listen to yourself. Don't listen to your fears, your anxieties, and your many doubts. When your self says that God is against you, when your self mutters that *life is out of control*, respond by preaching something like this to yourself:

> Father, thank you for sending your Son to be my great High Priest. Thank you for receiving his blood, shed on my behalf. Thank you for giving him all power and authority over my circumstances. Thank you for listening to his intercessions on my behalf. Now I rest in your goodness and the absolute sovereignty that you entrusted to your Son. I trust you for the past. I trust you for the future. I have nothing to fear. Christ

intercedes for me at your right hand, and he is always for me. He is never against me.

Discussion Questions

1. In your own words, what was this chapter about?

2. What was your favorite quote?

3. What circumstances in your personal life or in history have shaken your confidence in God's goodness and sovereignty? Why?

4. What does it sound like when your self is speaking to you?

5. What would it look like to preach the doctrine of the ascension to yourself?

Further Reading

- Blanchard, John. *Where Is God When Things Go Wrong?* Darlington, UK: Evangelical Press, 2005.

- Carson, D. A. *How Long, O Lord?: Reflections on Suffering and Evil.* Grand Rapids: Baker, 1990.

- Grudem, Wayne. *Systematic Theology: An Introduction to Biblical Doctrine.* Grand Rapids: Zondervan, 1994. See esp. chap. 28, "Resurrection and Ascension."

- Larkin, W. J., Jr. "Ascension." In *Dictionary of the Later New Testament and Its Developments*, edited by Ralph P. Martin and Peter H. Davids. Downers Grove, IL: IVP Academic, 1997.

- Watson, Thomas. *A Body of Divinity.* 1692. Reprint, Edinburgh, UK: Banner of Truth, 1958. See esp. part IV, chap. 7, "Christ's Exaltation."

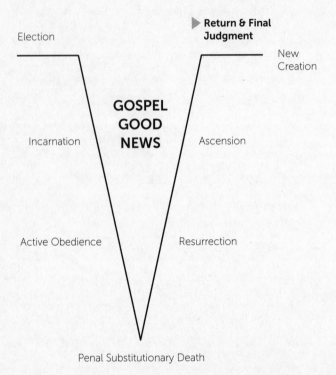

8

Christ Will Return

Complacency can be a problem. Many Christians are seriously unmotivated. They lack a sense of urgency. "A generation goes, and a generation comes, but the earth remains forever," observes Solomon (Eccl. 1:4). He continues:

The sun rises, and the sun goes down,
and hastens to the place where it rises.
The wind blows to the south
and goes around to the north;
around and around goes the wind,
and on its circuits the wind returns. (Eccl. 1:5–6)

Solomon put into words the humdrum of daily life. Its regularity can anesthetize us. The sun rises and sets. The seasons predictably come and go. It all happens with great consistency. All of this can put us into a spiritual slumber, numbing us to the cataclysmic events predicted by the Bible, diluting our sense of spiritual urgency.

This is the mind-set of the scoffer. "Where is the promise of his coming?" he asks. "For ever since the fathers fell asleep, all things are continuing as they were from the beginning of creation" (2 Peter 3:4).

Believers can succumb to the same attitude. It occurs when we forget that "the heavens and earth that now exist are stored up for fire, being kept until the day of judgment and destruction of the ungodly" (2 Peter 3:7).

In addition to life's regularity, the grace that comes to us through the gospel can numb us to the reality that these truths point to, leaving us careless about how we conduct our daily life—even causing us to abuse God's grace.

I used to have a friend, whom I will call Mark. He lived with Judy and me for a few months. He was utterly unmotivated. Mark didn't work consistently. When he did, it was often part-time. He had several graduate degrees, but that didn't motivate him either. He was dirty and unkempt. Tragically, he was as unmotivated in the spiritual world as in the business world. His Christianity was all grace and rest. There was no spiritual sweat on his brow. His motto was "Let go and let God," and he was good at the "letting go" part.

Mark lacked motivation. He lacked motivation because he lacked a clear conviction about Christ's second coming and the truths wrapped up in it—truths like the resurrection of the dead and the final judgment. These are the subjects of this chapter, and blessed is the believer who preaches them to himself or herself daily.

A proper conviction about the second coming of Christ motivates the unmotivated. When I was a new Christian, in the 1970s, the Jesus People felt this urgency. Their favorite expression was "Maranatha," which is Greek for "Come, Lord Jesus!" They expected the Lord to come any day, and they were eager for it to happen. It motivated them. They evangelized aggressively. They felt a burning desire to live godly lives and share the good news.

Christ may or may not come in our lifetime, but he will come eventually, and when he does, it will be to establish his kingly authority on earth. It will happen when we least expect it, and it will radically interrupt the predictability of life.

In the last chapter, we learned that Christ ascended to heaven to receive all power and authority. He ascended to sit on his throne and reign. He reigns from heaven, and he will do so until he has subjugated his foes. Then he will return to raise the dead and execute judgment. Every knee will bow and every tongue will confess that "Jesus Christ is Lord, to the glory of God the Father" (see Phil. 2:10–11). This is a sobering reality, and God designed this reality to infuse us with a sense of spiritual urgency. Why? His coming will signal the resurrection of the dead and the final judgment.

It is easy to doubt Christ's return. Because it will involve the overturning of nature's laws, to many it seems fantastic. But the return of Christ must occur. It is like the last chapter, the culmination of a great story. Without Christ's return, history would be like a novel that ended with the lovers going their separate ways. In other words, without Christ's literal return, the story that began in Eden will not have a happy ending.

Here is a quick summary of the story. We discussed it in the last chapter. God created the universe perfect. He created Adam, gave him dominion, and commanded him to rule. When Adam sinned, God withdrew that authority and gave it to a second Adam, Jesus Christ. At the cross, Jesus showed us what his servant-authority looks like. It dies for those it governs. It is a dying authority.

On the basis of his humility, Jesus ascended into heaven to receive all power and authority. Since that time, he has governed human history. His last enemy is death, and Christ will conquer it by raising the dead. Then he will pronounce judgment on all men. God's initial plan, described in Genesis 1 and 2, will have come full circle. Sin will be destroyed, all rebellion will be vanquished, immortality will be restored, and a man will once again exercise God's dominion on earth.

The second coming will involve three events. First, Christ will return. Second, he will raise the dead. Third, he will execute the final judgment.

IMAGINING CHRIST'S RETURN

The literary figure Goethe (1749–1832) said, "Few people have the imagination for reality."[1] By this he meant that ultimate reality is so great that few have the imagination to take it in. This describes most Christians, and our failure to exercise our imagination impoverishes our spiritual experience.

God has given us an imagination to aid our spiritual growth. In his book *The Enemy Within*, Kris Lundgaard gives us a layman's abridgement of *Sin and Temptation*, a classic work of the great Puritan divine, John Owen (1616–1683).[2] Owen knew that imagination is either a weapon to help us or a tool to amplify sin's seductions. In other words, that upon which we fix our imagination will tend to control us. For this reason, wise saints read the Bible with an active imagination, meditating on what they have read throughout the day. This is also why the Bible gives us many graphic images of key past and future events. God wants us to constantly imagine ultimate reality.

Scripture gives us graphic word pictures of Christ's coming to stir up our imaginations with hope and sobriety. We find one in Luke's account of Jesus' ascension. As the apostles watch Jesus ascend into heaven, two angels appear and say, "Men of Galilee, why do you stand looking into heaven? This Jesus, who was taken up from you into heaven, will come in the same way as you saw him go into heaven" (Acts 1:11). In other words, just as he ascended bodily on clouds, accompanied by angels, so he will return bodily on the clouds, accompanied by angels. His return will differ in one way, however. It will be not with one or two angels, but with thousands (see Dan. 7:10; Jude 14).

1 Thessalonians 4:16–17 adds more details.

The Lord himself will descend from heaven with a cry of command, with the voice of an archangel, and with the sound of the trumpet of God. And the dead in Christ will rise first. Then we who are alive, who are left, will be caught up together with them in the clouds to meet the Lord in the air.

Paul writes in another place,

The Lord Jesus [will be] revealed from heaven with his mighty angels in *flaming fire*, inflicting *vengeance* on those who do not know God and on those who do not obey the gospel of our Lord Jesus. They will suffer the punishment of eternal destruction, away from the presence of the Lord and from the glory of his might, when he comes on that day to be glorified in his saints, and to be marveled at among all who have believed. (2 Thess. 1:7–10)

These texts are a banquet for our imaginations. First, he will come bodily on clouds:

Clouds and thick darkness are all around him;
    righteousness and justice are the foundation of his throne.
Fire goes before him
    and burns up his adversaries all around. (Ps. 97:2–3)

His return will be earthshaking, hot, and noisy. He will thunder a command, the voice of the archangels will roar, and the trumpets of God will split the air. How many decibels will this be? Enough to shake all things to their foundations. We have all pulled up to a stoplight, only to have the bass from another car rattle our rearview mirror. This rattling is insignificant compared to the shaking that will accompany the cry of the archangel at Christ's return. "Yet once more I will *shake* not only the earth but also the heavens" (Heb. 12:26).

At Lazarus's tomb, Christ shouted, "Lazarus, come out" (John 11:43). Life surged into the dead man's corpse; he arose and obeyed. Jesus' command to Lazarus foreshadows the greater command that he will utter at his return. "The trumpet will sound, and the dead will be raised imperishable" (1 Cor. 15:52).

His word of authority will crack open the tombs, reconstitute our physical bodies, and resurrect the dead. First the saints who have died will rise. Then the saints who are alive will rise to join them and meet their Master in the air. Think of this happening to millions of souls at once, the ground tearing and wrenching, the cosmos groaning at the omnipotent command of Christ as he rips away the shroud of death forever.

Second Thessalonians also mentions "flaming fire." Think of a cosmic blowtorch or flamethrower. Remember, God knows heat. He made the sun and turned it up to 10,000 degrees Fahrenheit (at its surface temperature—it is 27,000,000 degrees at its core). Paul's prediction in 2 Thessalonians is grounded in texts like Psalm 50:3–4.

> Our God comes; he does not keep silence;
>> before him is a *devouring fire*,
>> around him a *mighty tempest*.
> He calls to the heavens above
>> and to the earth, that he may judge his people.

The prophet Daniel concurs.

> Thrones were placed, and the Ancient of days took his seat; his clothing was white as snow, and the hair of his head like pure wool; his throne was fiery flames; its wheels were burning fire. A *stream of fire* issued and came out from before him; a thousand thousands served him, and ten thousand times ten thousand stood before him; the court sat in judgment, and the books were opened. (Dan. 7:9–10)

Why are these biblical descriptions so graphic? God wants us to think hard, to think with our imaginations about eternal realities and then preach them to ourselves daily.

The second and third events will occur immediately after Christ's coming. They are the resurrection and the final judgment. These two events will complete our salvation. We often ask friends, "Are you saved?" By that we mean, "Are you reconciled to God through faith in the atoning work of Jesus Christ?" But we are never really saved until we have persevered to the end, experienced the resurrection of our bodies, and been justified at the final judgment. Ultimately, that is what it means to be "saved."

First, the resurrection.

RESURRECTION

Resurrection is a crucial gospel doctrine, and we already discussed it in chapter 6. As I write, one of the men in my church is recovering from a liver failure that almost took his life. One of our women just lost both her breasts to cancer. One of our young men just endured six months of chemotherapy for the second time. We live in a fallen world. In the words of Cornelius Plantinga, things are "not the way they are supposed to be."[3] As we saw in chapter 6, death, aging, and disease are not part of God's final plan. They are his deadly enemies, yet they are symptoms of a fallen world. "The last enemy to be destroyed is death" (1 Cor. 15:26).

Our salvation will not be complete until immortality has swallowed up death. That is the whole point of the resurrection. Resurrection life begins at the new birth, but it culminates when Christ raises our bodies. "He who raised Christ Jesus from the dead will also give life to your mortal bodies through his Spirit who dwells in you" (Rom. 8:11).

Jesus' return will initiate immortality. "For the trumpet will sound, and the dead will be raised imperishable, and we shall be changed" (1 Cor. 15:52).

Everyone, believer and unbeliever, will be raised. For the saints, this will mean joy. The pleasures of eternity will not just be spiritual. As we have seen, our joys will also be intellectual, emotional, social, and physical. By contrast, for unbelievers, the resurrection will mean suffering in the soul and also the body. This is what Jesus meant when he said, "An hour is coming when all who are in the tombs will hear his voice and come out, those who have done good to the resurrection of life, and those who have done evil to the resurrection of judgment" (John 5:28–29).

This takes us to the third and last drama of Christ's return, the final judgment.

FINAL JUDGMENT

Because judgments are inescapable in this life, we should expect them after death also. Academic grades are a form of judgment. Annual employee reviews are judgments. The boss judges our performance, and we find out how we are doing. Olympic competitions terminate in judgments—bronze, silver, or gold. We can't live without judging and being judged.

In the same way, at the end of life, there is a final judgment, and no one is exempt. "It is appointed for man to die once, and after that comes judgment" (Heb. 9:27). Most thoughtful people agree with this. As we saw in chapter 4, what they do not agree with is God's standard. It is perfection, God's righteousness.

Scripture describes the final judgment in sobering detail.

> You are storing up wrath for yourself on the day of wrath when God's righteous judgment will be revealed.
> He will render to each one *according to his works*: to those who by patience in well-doing seek for glory and honor and immortality, he will give eternal life; but for those who are self-seeking and do not obey the truth, but obey unrighteousness, there will be *wrath and fury*. (Rom. 2:5–8)

Those two words, "wrath and fury," might be the most unsettling ever put on paper.

What will it be like to experience the "wrath and fury" of God? This is not a pleasant thought. This is the wrath and fury of omnipotence—that is, infinite power. It is also the wrath and fury of omniscience—absolute knowledge. Nothing is hidden from God. He sees every hidden detail of our lives. "I tell you," adds Jesus, "on the day of judgment people will give account for every careless word they speak" (Matt. 12:36).

God will judge everyone on the basis of his or her works. Warning the church at Corinth, Paul writes, "For we must all appear before the judgment seat of Christ, so that each one may receive what is due for what he has *done in the body*, whether good or evil" (2 Cor. 5:10). Then Paul conspicuously adds, "Therefore, *knowing the fear of the Lord*, we persuade others" (v. 11). The reality of future judgment caused even the great apostle to fear God. He clearly foresaw the accounting that all, even himself, will render on the last day. Therefore, Paul was anxious to produce works that evidenced faith. If Paul was anxious about final judgment, how much more should you and I be?

We see the same pattern in Matthew 25:31–46 and Revelation 20:11–15. In both cases, the judgment is according to works. "Truly, I say to you, as you did it to one of the least of these my brothers, you did it to me" (Matt. 25:40). "And the dead were judged by what was written in the books, according to *what they had done*" (Rev. 20:12).

You are probably thinking, "A judgment according to works? What happened to justification by faith alone?" That is an excellent question, and the answer is simple. We are justified by faith plus nothing. However, real faith is more than a mental tip of the hat to the creed. It is an "*assurance* of things hoped " and a "*conviction* of things not seen" (Heb. 11:1). If someone yells "fire" in a crowded theater, those with a conviction that he is telling the truth will head for the exits. But those with only a mental assent will remain in their seats. In the same way, because it is an assurance and a conviction, saving faith always produces good works.

This is James's point. "Faith by itself, if it does not have works, is dead" (James 2:17). In other words, a faith without works does not save. Why? Because it is not real faith.

It follows that the more works one has, the more faith. Our works point to the nature, depth, and quality of our faith. On the day of final judgment, God will reward us according to our faith as evidenced by our works. Believers and unbelievers will be judged according to their works, but in the case of believers, their works will point to the presence or absence of saving faith. Their faith, not their works, will save them. As we have already seen, God requires perfection. Since no one is perfect, works by themselves can save no one. We are saved by the imputation of Christ's works, as discussed in chapter 4.

That is why the final judgment energized even the apostle Paul. "Therefore, knowing the fear of the Lord, we persuade others" (2 Cor. 5:11).

Unbelievers will also be judged on their works, and since the standard is perfection, they will fall hopelessly short. Damnation will be the result.

The reality of the events accompanying Christ's return, the resurrection, and the final judgment shaped Paul's life and message. For example, when he was given a chance to testify to Felix, the governor, Paul reasoned about "righteousness, self-control, and the coming judgment" (Acts 24:25). When given a chance to witness to the Greek intelligentsia, Paul reminded them that God "has fixed a day on which he will judge the world in righteousness by a man whom he has appointed; and of this he has given assurance to all by raising him from the dead" (Acts 17:31).

Is this the gospel we share with unbelievers? Is it the gospel we preach to ourselves?

SO WHAT?

Let's close this chapter with three exhortations.

The first exhortation is to be ready. Jesus did not emphasize knowing the time of his coming. Rather, he repeatedly stressed that no one would know the time or day. "Therefore you also must be ready, for the Son of Man is coming at an hour you do not expect" (Matt. 24:44). Then, in the next chapter, just to make sure we didn't miss it, Jesus says it again: "Watch therefore, for you know neither the day nor the hour" (Matt. 25:13).

Since the time of his return was unknown, Jesus and the apostles emphasized readiness. Readiness means a life of growing holiness and godliness, a life testifying to the presence of genuine, saving faith.

Was my friend, Mark, ready? I don't know. He certainly wasn't concerned about it, but he should have been. He needed the sense of urgency that comes to those who preach the truth of Christ's return, including the resurrection and the final judgment, to themselves on a regular basis.

The second exhortation is be joyful. Christ's return means the completion of our salvation. It means resurrected bodies completely liberated from the effects of death, aging, and disease. It means a new heaven and a new earth. It means justification for all who believe. They will hear these wonderful words: "Well done, good and faithful servant." On the basis of our faith in his active obedience, Jesus will usher us into eternal glory.

The third exhortation is be sober. Watch your life and your doctrine. Make sure that your faith is saving faith. "And the dead were judged by what was written in the books, according to what they had done. . . . If anyone's name was not found written in the book of life, he was thrown into the lake of fire" (Rev. 20:12, 15). True grace produces works. It produces the works that point to saving faith.

> For the grace of God has appeared . . . *training* us to renounce ungodliness and worldly passions, and to live self-controlled, upright, and godly lives in the present age, waiting for our blessed hope, the appearing of the glory of our great God and Savior Jesus Christ. (Titus 2:11–13)

Christ's return, the resurrection, and the final judgment should inform every waking moment of our existence. They will do this to those who preach these things to themselves daily. For example, parenting is about preparing our children for the final judgment. One overlooked end of marriage is helping our spouse prepare for the final judgment. One crucial purpose of our life together as a local church is helping each other prepare for Christ's coming, the resurrection, and the final judgment. Let us pray with the Puritans, "May I view all things in the mirror of eternity, waiting for the coming of my Lord, listening for the last trumpet call, hastening unto the new heaven and earth."

CONCLUSION

What would it look like to preach this truth to oneself? It might look something like this.

Father, thank you for sending your Son to die for my sins and rise again. Father, I long for Christ's return in glory. It will be the day of my reward. He will come on the clouds of heaven, with thousands of mighty angels, with rivers of fire preceding him. The trumpet will sound, the dead will rise, and Christ will render final judgment. I will stand before you to be judged by my deeds. They will reveal whether I really believed or if it was all smoke and mirrors. On that day, the books will be opened, and my deeds will speak for the nature and extent of my faith. God, give me a sense of urgency about this day. Give me a biblical hope in the coming reward.

Discussion Questions

1. In your own words, what was this chapter about?
2. What was your favorite quote?
3. Which text of Scripture concerning the second coming struck you most vividly?
4. In what way did this chapter change your understanding of the resurrection of the dead?

5. How did this chapter change your understanding of the final judgment?

6. Give an example of how you would preach these truths to yourself.

Further Reading

- Grudem, Wayne. *Systematic Theology: An Introduction to Biblical Doctrine*. Grand Rapids: Zondervan, 1994. See esp. chaps. 54, "The Return of Christ: When and How?," 56, "The Final Judgment and Eternal Punishment," and 42, "Glorification (Receiving a Resurrection Body)."

- Helm, Paul. *The Last Things: Death, Judgment, Heaven, and Hell*. Edinburgh, UK: Banner of Truth, 1989.

- Hoekema, Anthony A. *The Bible and the Future*. Grand Rapids: Eerdmans, 1979.

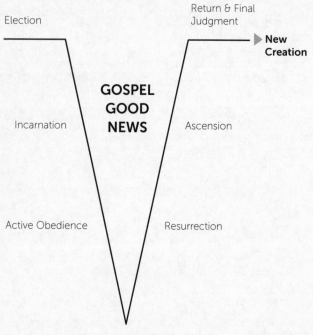

9

A New Creation

No account of the gospel is complete without a discussion of its culmination, the new creation.

Before my conversion, and even for a few years after, I imagined that heaven was a place far removed—somewhere out in space, with angels and people floating on clouds and plucking harps. It didn't sound that interesting, except for the fact that Christ was there. Maybe your experience has been like mine. It is hard to get excited about a heaven like that. Our sensory pleasures are connected to daily physical life. My idea of heaven was neither "daily" nor "physical." I have good news. This is not the biblical view of heaven. Heaven is a place. It is the new creation.

Randy Alcorn explains,

> Everything pleasurable we know about life on Earth we have experienced through our senses. So, when Heaven is portrayed as beyond the reach of our senses, it doesn't invite us; instead, it alienates and even frightens us. . . . In order to get a picture of Heaven—which will one day be centered on the New Earth—you don't need to look up at the clouds; you simply need to look around you and imagine what all this would be like without sin and death and suffering and corruption.[1]

Although this is true, we need to include an important caveat. Heaven is wherever God is. After the sin with the golden

111

calf, God told Moses that he was not going to accompany him into the Promised Land. "Go up to a land flowing with milk and honey; but I will not go up among you, lest I consume you on the way, for you are a stiff necked people" (Ex. 33:3). But Moses responded, "If your presence will not go with me, do not bring us up from here" (Ex. 33:15). In other words, the presence of God was so valuable to Moses that he would rather stay in the howling wilderness with God than go into the land of milk and honey without him.

This is how we should think about heaven. Heaven is wherever God is. It is the presence of God that makes Paradise a paradise. Yes, heaven is a new creation. Someday God will remove all the effects of sin from it. God will restore it to its original condition—unblemished by evil and death. Although the new creation will then be heaven, it is the sweet presence of God that makes it so. It will not be the presence of spouses, relatives, children, or a new physical world. These will all contribute, but the presence of the living God is always the main ingredient of heaven.

The present creation has been affected by Adam's sin. But even in its fallen state, creation can be breathtakingly beautiful. I recently drove to the top of Steptoe Butte, a prominence in eastern Washington that juts up out of the Palouse, one of the most fertile wheat-growing areas in the world. From the summit, golden wheat fields roll off toward the west as far as the eye can see. To the east, the rolling hills rise to eventually become the Rocky Mountains. At sunset on a summer evening, the view is a God-glorifying treat. One is tempted to think, How can anything be more beautiful than this? But the whole point of our future hope is that this creation, even on its best day, is a badly corrupted version of what God initially created and also of what is to come.

The important lesson is this: sin doesn't affect just people. It affects everything that God put under Adam's stewardship.

This means that this world, on its most beautiful day, is like a beautiful woman stumbling out of bed in the morning with greasy hair, bad breath, and no makeup. Although her potential for beauty is obvious, at 6 a.m. she is not at her best. In the same way, the world today has a certain inherent beauty, but it is not what it is supposed to be.

Paul understood these limitations. "The creation itself will be set free from its bondage to corruption and obtain the freedom of the glory of the children of God. For we know that the whole creation has been groaning together in the pains of childbirth until now" (Rom. 8:21–22). The cosmos (creation) has been "subjected to futility" (v. 20). God subjected it. The subjection is part of the curse that followed Adam's sin. Creation is in bondage to decay and death, and it groans to be released, to return to normalcy. In other words, by biblical standards, the present creation is woefully substandard.

Creation's restoration to God's original intention will be the place we call *heaven*. That means that heaven is a physical place. It is not angels on clouds. God created the physical world for his glory. It was both a tabernacle for his presence and a residence for Adam and Eve. Since God created Adam and Eve immortal, they would not have died and then gone to a place called heaven. The earth was their eternal home. What made the earth so heavenly was the direct presence of God, mediated by the Holy Spirit to men and women unsullied by sin. In other words, the physical world, as God created it, was a utopia before sin, decay, death, suffering, and aging became part of it because of the fall.

However, sin drove heaven from earth and made earth a suburb of hell. The unimpeded, unquenchable pleasure that God intended went with it. This explains why it is easier to imagine hell than heaven. Heaven is a place without suffering or pain. "He will wipe away every tear from their eyes, and death shall be no more, neither shall there be mourning nor crying nor pain anymore, for the former things have passed away" (Rev. 21:4). A stressless life without suffering and pain is not our daily experience. By contrast, because tears, death, mourning, stress, and pain are all common to our daily experience, the pain and suffering of hell are easy to imagine.

THE EARTH CURSED

When God cursed the ground, the cosmos also came under judgment. "And to Adam [God] said, '. . . *cursed is the ground* because of you; in pain you shall eat of it all the days of your life; thorns and thistles it shall bring forth for you'" (Gen. 3:17–18). Because of God's curse, the cosmos and the earth resist us.

The earth resists cultivation. For example, only about 11 percent of the world's land mass is arable. Even the small percent that is arable is subject to occasional drought, freezing, flooding, and other destructive weather patterns. The other 89 percent is too mountainous, cold, hot, or arid for cultivation.[2] I don't think the earth has always been this way. For example, the vast coal reserves under the North and South Poles and the Sahara Desert testify that they were all once verdant with vegetation. Is the paucity of arable land a by-product of the curse?

Not only does the earth resist cultivation, it can also be deadly. The Boxing Day tsunami of 2004 in Southeast Asia killed three hundred thousand people. A March 2011 tsunami wreaked havoc on the northeastern coast of Japan, killing roughly twenty thousand people. At the time of this writing, the northeastern United States is recovering from billions of dollars of damage caused by Hurricane Sandy.

Earthquakes, hurricanes, volcanoes, blizzards, drought, insects, agricultural diseases, and adverse weather patterns are just a few of the symptoms of God's curse on the ground. But there is good news. God has not given up on his initial plan. He has a rescue plan, and he has put it in motion.

RESTORATION PROPHESIED

God has not made this plan a secret. The Scriptures describing it are numerous. After his resurrection and before his ascension, Jesus spent forty days on earth. He taught his disciples about the kingdom of God. He explained his plan to restore all things. We know this because a few months later, Peter preached about Jesus, "whom heaven must receive until the time for *restoring* all the things about which God spoke by the mouth of his holy prophets long ago" (Acts 3:21). In other words, the restoration of creation will come, but not until Christ returns.

The prophets predicted this? When did they do that, and what did they say about it? "The heavens vanish like smoke," wrote Isaiah, "the earth will wear out like a garment, and they who dwell in it will die in like manner; but my salvation will be forever, and my righteousness will never be dismayed" (Isa. 51:6). Isaiah foresaw the end of the earth as we know it and its replacement with one freed from the curse of sin and death. "For behold, I create new heavens and a new earth, and the former things shall not be remembered or come into mind" (Isa. 65:17).[3]

One of the clearest and most unambiguous predictions appears in the third chapter of Peter's second letter.

> But the day of the Lord will come like a thief, and then the heavens will pass away with a roar, and the heavenly bodies will be burned up and dissolved, and the earth and the works that are done on it will be exposed. . . .
> But according to his promise we are waiting for new heavens and a new earth in which righteousness dwells. (2 Peter 3:10, 13)

HEAVEN ON EARTH

As we have seen, it is almost impossible to imagine a world without aging, sickness, and death, without bitterness or hurt feelings, without selfishness, misunderstandings, and depression, without wars or bad days. The new creation will be a world without tornadoes, hurricanes, or droughts, accompanied by abundant arable land eagerly cooperating to produce copious harvests of grain and fruit. This is the biblical idea of heaven, and the best news is that it will be realized right here on a refashioned planet, purified of sin and all of its effects. God will restore the lady's beauty. She will bathe, put on makeup, and dress for a wedding (Rev. 21:1–5).

The new creation will be about spiritual and physical joys and pleasures that we now experience only briefly. Today they come and go, but someday we will experience them in a highly amplified, sustained state. The joys of carefully prepared food, good wine, bathing, sleeping, working, friendship, athletics, accomplishment, and so on will all be ours, in a superlative form. It will all be wonderful because Christ will dwell with us, immediately perceptible at all times, in a way only fleetingly experienced today. In the words of Anthony Hoekema, "Since God will make the new earth his dwelling place, and since where God dwells there heaven is, we shall then continue to be in heaven while we are on the new earth. For heaven and earth will then no longer be separated, as they are now, but will be one (see Rev. 21:1–3)."[4]

ALREADY, BUT NOT YET

When will all this occur? In the chapter on the resurrection, we introduced the expression "already, but not yet."[5] It applies both to the resurrection and to the new creation. The new creation has already begun, but its consummation awaits the future. In the words of the great apostle, "For the present form of this world is passing away" (1 Cor. 7:31; note the present tense). D. A. Carson writes, "The tension between the 'already' and the 'not yet'—the kingdom has already arrived, and the kingdom has not yet come—is a commonplace of biblical thought."[6]

In what way is the new creation "already?" The new creation began with Christ's resurrection. He was "the firstborn of all creation" (Col. 1:15). The primary idea behind "firstborn" is "firstborn in importance."[7] But a secondary idea is "firstborn in time." His resurrection began to turn back the curse of sin and death. Its first manifestation was Jesus' glorified body, an immortal body fit for a new creation, a body pointing us to the hope for which we eagerly wait.

As we have already seen, the second stage in the "already" begins when believers experience new birth. New birth is a down payment on the world to come. "Down payment" refers to a growing experience of the spiritual pleasures of the world to come. The primary pleasure is fellowship with God on the basis of his Son's atonement and made real by the power of the Holy Spirit. So Paul, with this in mind, writes, "If anyone is in Christ, he is a new creation. The old has passed away; behold, the new has come" (2 Cor. 5:17).

The down payment is an experience of the joys of the world to come. "In him you also . . . were sealed with the promised Holy Spirit, who is the guarantee [down payment] of our inheritance until we acquire possession of it, to the praise of his glory" (Eph. 1:13–14). The Holy Spirit is both the down payment and the seal. All true Christians have experienced and are experiencing the down payment. Its is a foretaste of heaven, of life in the new creation. The Spirit's presence in our lives testifies that the new creation has begun and that we are beginning to experience it.

"Participating in resurrection life" and "being made a new creation" are two ways of saying the same thing. Under the heading "Already, but Not Yet" in chapter 6, we discussed what it means to experience resurrection life. Since it is the same thing as participating in the new creation, I will not repeat what I wrote there.

The bottom line is this. If the Holy Spirit has made you a new creation, the powers of the age to come have broken into your present experience. This is evidenced by your faith

in Christ, hunger to obey God, love for his word, and a growing sense of God's presence. You are tasting the firstfruits
of immortality.

The new creation will come fully only after Christ returns.
Christ will re-create the cosmos. He will create a "place" that
is fit for all who have embraced the gospel through faith and
repentance. Summing it up, Edith Humphrey writes,

> All that we call nature is no mere backdrop for our lives, but
> a reality of which we are, and will remain, a part. We will not
> become disembodied spirits, but will retain that link with the
> material world that God has declared to be 'good'—Though there
> will be more substance and glory than we can now imagine. . . .
> A firm grasp on the new creation will instruct us not to dispar-
> age the body, not to leash the Spirit of God, and not to despise
> the world that God has made. . . . Salvation is recognized as
> having an immensely broad scope. Thus, we learn to be grate-
> ful not simply for our rescue from sin, but for the singing hope
> of a new creation.[8]

SO WHAT?

Why does this matter? Does this truth help me anywhere
else? Yes!

First, it reminds us that creation and God are separate enti-
ties. If God is the Creator, then the creation is something apart
from him. This is important because pantheism teaches the
opposite. It is the belief that God and creation are one. In his
book *Miracles*, C. S. Lewis notes that pantheism is the religion
to which cultures usually succumb when Christianity grows
weak. Hinduism, Buddhism, and Taoism are fundamentally
pantheistic. In addition, the contemporary environmental movement has pantheistic overtones.

The Christian hope is different. God dwells apart from
and above nature. He made it, he existed before it, and he
exists apart from it. This means that, although we need to

be good stewards of our environment, we do not worship it. For Christians, the environment is not something to serve. It is a gift from God. The environment exists to serve us, not vice versa. This is increasingly not the conviction of contemporary culture. A recent Google search for the word *guilt* brought up several pages of references, but they were mostly feelings of guilt about how we treat the environment. Guilt is decreasingly about our attitude toward the God of the Bible and increasingly about our attitude toward the common street god, the environment. Pantheism is alive and well in the Western world, and it signals a revival of ancient paganism.

The second lesson is that material things are inherently good. "And God saw everything that he had made, and behold, *it was very good*" (Gen. 1:31). That is why God plans to restore it. He likes the material world. This also means that physical pleasures are good. Physical beauty is good. The human body is good. Food, sex, wine, houses, furniture, vacations, and vehicles—they are all good. This means that it is not money that is the root of all evil, but rather the *love* of money (1 Tim. 6:10).

The Greek philosophers taught something altogether different. Many of them believed that spiritual things were inherently good, but that material things (bodies, food, drink, etc.) were inherently evil. This idea has infiltrated Western culture. More importantly, it has infiltrated the church. It explains our antipathy toward alcoholic drink. It explains the medieval revulsion toward sex, even marriage. Most importantly, it explains our anti-material views of heaven. These we need to repudiate. We need to exult with God, "It is very good."

The third lesson is that this short life is not ultimate. If God has prepared for each of us an eternity of "joy that is inexpressible and filled with glory" (1 Peter 1:8), then what difference does it make whether I get to the top of the corporate ladder? Does it matter whether my children go to Ivy League schools? Does it really matter that I lose those extra ten pounds, that I can afford that vacation to Mexico, or that I jog those fifteen miles this week? Meditation on the world to come puts all these in their proper perspective. All that really matters is that I do all things for the glory of God (1 Cor. 10:31).

Last, this chapter matters reminds us that salvation is cosmic. It is about much more than our personal conversion. It is about much more than the health of our families or the growth of our local church. It is about the redemption of the entire cosmos. In the words of the *Holman Illustrated Bible Dictionary*, "The biblical hope for mankind is tied to the conviction that persons cannot be completely set free from the power of sin apart from the redemption of the created order—earth as well as the heavens."[9] Never forget that "the redemption accomplished by Christ culminates in a new creation."[10]

CONCLUSION

Peter exhorts us, "Set your hope fully on the grace that will be brought to you at the revelation of Jesus Christ" (1 Peter 1:13). We do this when we talk back to ourselves—when we preach to ourselves, rather than listening to ourselves.

How would someone preach this truth to himself or herself? It might look something like this.

Father, I exult in the hope of a new creation. Heaven will be a physical world. Heaven will be on earth. On its most beautiful day, this creation is a paltry edition of what is coming. I thank you for physical pleasures. I thank you for food, wine, family, feasting, work, vocation, and sleep. But most of all I thank you for your Son, who loved me and gave himself up for me.

Amen!

Discussion Questions

1. In your own words, try to sum up the main point of this chapter.

2. What was your favorite quote in this chapter? Why?

3. Before reading this chapter, what did heaven mean to you?

4. When theologians use the expression "already, but not yet" with reference to the new creation, what do they have in mind?

5. How have you experienced the "already" of the new creation?

6. What would it sound like to preach to yourself about the future?

7. What circumstances would prompt you to preach this truth to yourself?

Further Reading

- Alcorn, Randy. *Heaven*. Wheaton, IL: Tyndale, 2004.

- Grudem, Wayne. *Systematic Theology: An Introduction to Biblical Doctrine*. Grand Rapids: Zondervan, 1994. See esp. chap. 57, "The New Heavens and New Earth."

- Milne, Bruce. *The Message of Heaven and Hell*. Downers Grove, IL: InterVarsity Press, 2002.

Notes

Chapter One: Preach to Yourself

1. D. Martyn Lloyd-Jones, *Spiritual Depression: Its Causes and Its Cure* (Grand Rapids: Eerdmans, 1965), 20.

2. Jerry Bridges, *The Discipline of Grace: God's Role and Our Role in the Pursuit of Holiness* (Colorado Springs: NavPress, 2006), 59.

3. Jerry Bridges and Bob Bevington, *The Great Exchange: My Sin for His Righteousness* (Wheaton, IL: Crossway, 2007), 42.

4. Jeff Purswell, "What Precisely Is the Gospel?," *C. J.'s View from the Cheap Seats* (blog), *Sovereign Grace Ministries*, October 22, 2009, http://www.sovereigngraceministries.org/blogs/cj-mahaney/post/what-is-the-gospel-jeff-purswell.aspx.

5. D. R. W. Wood, ed., *New Bible Dictionary*, 3rd ed. (Downers Grove, IL: InterVarsity Press, 1996), 426.

6. For example, although the gospel is the good news that God's kingdom has come (Matt. 4:23; Mark 1:14–15), it also has a past emphasis. It was first proclaimed in the garden of Eden (Gen. 3:15), and Galatians 3:8 tells us that Abraham heard it (in Gen. 12:1–3). In 1 Corinthians 15, it includes Christ's death and resurrection. In 1 Timothy 3:16 and 2 Timothy 1:10, it includes the incarnation. But it also includes the future. In Romans 2:16, it includes the final judgment. In Colossians 1:23 it is about future hope, and in 2 Timothy 1:10 it is about future immortality. It includes glorification in 2 Thessalonians 2:14.

7. See a discussion of this subject in James M. Hamilton Jr., *God's Glory in Salvation through Judgment: A Biblical Theology* (Wheaton, IL: Crossway, 2010), 37–66.

8. For a detailed examination of this statement, see Jonathan Edwards, "Concerning the End for Which God Created the World," in *Two Dissertations* (Boston: S. Kneeland, 1765), available online at http://www.monergism.com/dissertation-concerning-end-which-god-created-world-jonathan-edwards. For the same text with an excellent

four-chapter introduction, see John Piper, *God's Passion for His Glory: Living the Vision of Jonathan Edwards* (Wheaton, IL: Crossway, 1998).

9. Bridges, *The Discipline of Grace*, 109.

10. Edward T. Welch, *When People Are Big and God Is Small: Overcoming Peer Pressure, Codependency, and the Fear of Man* (Phillipsburg, NJ: P&R, 1997), 146.

11. Paul David Tripp, *Dangerous Calling: Confronting the Unique Challenges of Pastoral Ministry* (Wheaton, IL: Crossway, 2012), 99.

12. John Piper, "Never Let the Gospel Get Smaller," *Desiring God*, March 17, 2009, http://www.desiringgod.org/Blog/1687_never_let_the_gospel_get_smaller.

13. Mark Dever, *Nine Marks of a Healthy Church* (Wheaton, IL: Crossway, 2000), 81.

Chapter Two: Chosen before the Foundation of the World

1. See Romans 9:6–24. Here are a few texts that describe God's selectively revealing himself: Amos 8:11–12; Matt. 11:25–27; 13:11; 16:17; Luke 19:42; 24:16, 31, 45; John 1:12–13; 5:21; 6:39; 9:39; 2 Cor. 3:14; 1 Peter 2:9.

God chose Israel. See Deut. 4:20, 37–39; 7:6–7; 14:2; 1 Sam. 12:22; Ps. 135:4; Isa. 41:8; 43:20–21; 64:8; Ezek. 20:5; Zech. 2:10–12; Luke 10:21–24; Rom. 9:10–11.

God chose the Gentiles. See Matt. 11:25; 22:14; Luke 10:21–24; John 6:37, 39; 10:16, 26; 13:18; 17:6, 9, 24; Rom. 8:28–33; 11:4–7; 1 Cor. 1:26–31; Eph. 1:4, 11; James 1:18; 2:5; 1 Peter 2:9; 2 Peter 1:10.

God chose us to display his free mercy and grace. See Ex. 33:19; Matt. 19:30; 20:16; Rom. 9:14–15.

2. Elisha Coles, quoted in Iain Murray, "The Puritans and the Doctrine of Election," in *The Puritan Papers*, vol. 1, *1956–1959*, ed. J. I. Packer (Phillipsburg, NJ: P&R, 2000), 7.

3. Murray, "The Puritans and the Doctrine of Election," 9.

4. D. A. Carson, *The Difficult Doctrine of the Love of God* (Wheaton, IL: Crossway, 2000), 18.

Chapter Three: The Great Descent

1. William P. Farley, *Gospel-Powered Humility* (Phillipsburg, NJ: P&R, 2011).

2. Stuart Scott, *From Pride to Humility: A Biblical Perspective* (Bemidji, MN: Focus Publishing, 2000), 5.

3. A. W. Tozer, *The Knowledge of the Holy* (New York: Harper & Row, 1961), 51.

4. John Flavel, *Works* (1820; repr., Edinburgh: Banner of Truth, 1968), 1:226.

5. Thomas Watson, *A Body of Divinity* (1692; repr., Edinburgh: Banner of Truth, 1958), 192.

Chapter Four: No Hope without It!

1. Perfection is what God requires. See Isa. 33:14–16; Pss. 15; 24:3–5; 130:3; Matt. 5:20; Gal. 3:10–13; Heb. 7:11; 10:1, 14; 12:23; James 2:10–12.

2. Here are some other texts that refer to the imputation of Christ's righteousness: Rom. 1:16–17; 3:21–22; 4:3, 6; 5:17, 19; 10:4; 1 Cor. 1:30; 2 Cor. 3:9; 5:14–15; Gal. 2:19–21; Phil. 3:9.

3. Jerry Bridges and Bob Bevington, *The Great Exchange: My Sin for His Righteousness* (Wheaton, IL: Crossway, 2007), 82.

4. Roland H. Bainton, *Here I Stand: A Life of Martin Luther* (Nashville: Abingdon, 1950), 49.

Chapter Five: The Heart of the Matter

1. "Jared" is not one individual. He is a composite of several individuals with whom I have talked over the years.

Chapter Six: Hope for the Hopeless

1. Francis Bacon, "Of Death," in *Essays*, 1625, quoted in *The International Thesaurus of Quotations*, rev. ed., compiled by Eugene Ehrlich and Marshall De Bruhl (New York: HarperCollins, 1996), 143.

2. G. K. Beale develops this thought in *A New Testament Biblical Theology: The Unfolding of the Old Testament in the New* (Grand Rapids: Baker, 2011), 228.

3. In John 11, Jesus raises Lazarus. He raises the son of a widow in Nain in Luke 7, and he raises Jairus's daughter in Matthew 9.

Chapter Seven: The Forgotten Doctrine

1. Diarmaid MacCulloch, *The Reformation* (New York: Viking, 2003), 228–30.

2. Quoted in Peter Toon, "Resurrected and Ascended: The Exalted Christ," *Bibliotheca Sacra* 140 (1983): 195.

3. Philip W. Comfort and Walter A. Elwell, eds., *Tyndale Bible Dictionary* (Wheaton, IL: Tyndale House Publishers, 2001), 116.

Chapter Eight: Christ Will Return

1. Quoted in Carolyn Weber, *Surprised by Oxford: A Memoir* (Nashville: Thomas Nelson, 2011), 45.

2. Kris Lundgaard, *The Enemy Within: Straight Talk about the Power and Defeat of Sin* (Phillipsburg, NJ: P&R, 1998), chap. 8.

3. Cornelius Plantinga Jr., *Not the Way It's Supposed to Be: A Breviary of Sin* (Grand Rapids: Eerdmans, 1995).

Chapter Nine: A New Creation

1. Randy Alcorn, *Heaven* (Wheaton, IL: Tyndale, 2004), 17.

2. Navin Ramankutty, Amato T. Evan, Chad Monfreda, and Jonathan A. Foley, "Farming the Planet: 1. Geographic Distribution of Global Agricultural Lands in the Year 2000," *Global Biogeochemical Cycles* 22, no. 1 (March 2008), available online at http://onlinelibrary.wiley.com/doi/10.1029/2007GB002952/full.

3. Many other texts predict this hope. For example, see Ps. 102:25–26; Isa. 11:6–9; 66:22; Heb. 12:25–26; 2 Peter 3:1–13; Rev. 21:1.

4. Anthony A. Hoekema, *The Bible and the Future* (Grand Rapids: Eerdmans, 1979), 274.

5. See George Eldon Ladd, *The Presence of the Future: The Eschatology of Biblical Realism* (Grand Rapids: Eerdmans, 1974).

6. D. A. Carson, *How Long, Oh Lord?: Reflections on Suffering and Evil* (Grand Rapids: Baker, 1990), 136.

7. See Richard B. Gaffin Jr., *Resurrection and Redemption: A Study in Paul's Soteriology*, 2nd ed. (Phillipsburg, NJ: P&R, 1987), 37.

8. Edith M. Humphrey, "New Creation," in *Dictionary for Theological Interpretation of the Bible*, ed. Kevin J. Vanhoozer (Grand Rapids: Baker Academic, 2005), 537.

9. P. E. Robertson, "Heavens, New," in *Holman Illustrated Bible Dictionary*, ed. Chad Brand, Charles Draper, and Archie England (Nashville: Holman Bible Publishers, 2003), 734.

10. Philip W. Comfort and Walter A. Elwell, eds., *Tyndale Bible Dictionary* (Wheaton, IL: Tyndale House Publishers, 2001), 948.